EXPLORING ST. LOUIS, MISSOURI

A Comprehensive Guide to History, Culture, and Hidden Gems in the Heart of America

Merrick Crestwood

All rights reserved. No part of this publication may be reproduced, distributed, or transmitted in any form or by any means, including photocopying, recording, or other electronic or mechanical methods, without the prior written permission of the publisher, except in the case of brief quotations embodied in critical reviews and certain other noncommercial uses permitted by copyright law.

Copyright © Merrick Crestwood, 2024

Table of Contents

Preface — 5
Chapter 1 — 6
    Introduction to the Gateway City — 6
    Synopsis and Fast Facts — 8
    Best Times to Visit — 11
Chapter 2 — 15
    The Gateway Arch — 15
    Forest Park Attractions — 19
    Cathedral Basilica of Saint Louis — 24
Chapter 3 — 28
    City Museum — 28
    Missouri History Museum — 32
    National Blues Museum — 37
    Anheuser-Busch Brewery Tour — 42
Chapter 4 — 47
    St. Louis Zoo — 47
    The Magic House — 51
    Saint Louis Science Center — 56
Chapter 5 — 62
    The Delmar Loop — 62
    Soulard and the Farmers Market — 67
    Lafayette Square — 73
    Central West End — 77
Chapter 6 — 82
    Forest Park: Trails and Recreational Activities — 82
    Missouri Botanical Garden — 88
    Riverboat Cruises on the Mississippi — 94
Chapter 7 — 99
    Catching a Cardinals Game at Busch Stadium — 99
    The Fabulous Fox Theatre — 103

Chapter 8   108
    Must-Try Local Foods   108
    Best Places for Craft Beer and Cocktails   113
    Nightlife Hotspots and Bars   117

Chapter 9   121
    Getting Around St. Louis   121
    Accommodation Options   126
    Safety Tips and Traveler Resources   131

Preface

Here's to an exciting journey into the heart of America. Travelers of all stripes may enjoy a diverse range of experiences in St. Louis, a city that seamlessly connects the past and present. This guide will help you experience the charm and essence of this extraordinary location, whether you're coming back for a closer look or visiting for the first time.

Imagine yourself standing beneath the imposing Gateway Arch and enjoying the fresh Mississippi River breeze as you turn the pages of these pages. Imagine yourself meandering through Forest Park, where every turn reveals a fresh surprise, from striking artwork to fascinating zoo animals. In St. Louis, current culture flourishes in vibrant districts as history echoes from the walls of historic structures.

Not only are St. Louis's sights and attractions unique, but their backstories are as well. Locals take great pride in sharing their past via festivals, music, and cuisine. Like a quaint coffee shop or a bustling street market, it's the unanticipated delight of discovering a hidden gem.

More than a directory of locations to see is what this book seeks to be. It's a request to fully embrace St. Louis' unique vibe. Insider advice, first-hand stories, and useful information are scattered throughout the chapters to help you have an amazing trip. This city exudes warmth and hospitality, whether you're watching a game at Busch Stadium, admiring the mosaics in the Cathedral Basilica, or just nosing around on some delicious butter cake.

There is always something to treasure in St. Louis for visitors. Thus, let the magic of this city reveal itself to you and have an open mind to new encounters. Let's explore St. Louis's numerous aspects and create lasting experiences.

Chapter 1

Introduction to the Gateway City

A shining example of history, creativity, and cultural diversity is St. Louis. This energetic city, which is tucked away on the Mississippi River's western bank, has long been a vital hub for travelers, colonists, and idealists. It is still a peaceful melting pot of experiences where the old and modern cohabit today.

Reaching 630 feet into the sky, the magnificent Gateway Arch made of stainless steel dominates the city's skyline. This famous building, finished in 1965, honors the US government's westward migration and is a symbol of the pioneering nature that characterizes St. Louis. Beyond this architectural marvel, though, is a city full of legends, customs, and a distinct charm that enthralls everyone who visits.

The rich history of St. Louis began when French fur traders Pierre Laclède and Auguste Chouteau founded the city in 1764. Immediately after its founding, the city—named for French King Louis IX—became a thriving center of exploration and trade. The Louisiana Purchase in 1803 served as a crucial launching pad for the Lewis & Clark Expedition, solidifying its significance even further. You can still feel the legacy of these early explorers and the rich tapestry of cultures they contributed to as you stroll around the city's old neighborhoods.

There is something for everyone in the vibrant city of modern St. Louis. It has a lively artistic scene, beautiful parks, and top-notch museums. The Pulitzer Arts Foundation, the St. Louis Art Museum, and the Missouri History Museum provide an in-depth exploration of regional and worldwide stories. A feast for the senses is offered by performances by the St. Louis Symphony Orchestra and the Muny, the country's largest and oldest outdoor musical theater.

Forest Park, a vast 1,300-acre paradise that played host to the 1904 World's Fair, is one of the city's greatest jewels. These days, the Science Center, the Missouri History Museum, and the St. Louis Zoo—some of the city's most popular attractions—are housed there. A concert at the Muny, a stroll through its gardens, or a boat ride on its lakes—Forest Park is a place where memories are built.

St. Louis is a city of neighborhoods as well, and each one has a unique personality and taste. There is always something new to explore, from the vibrant energy of the Delmar Loop, which is renowned for its varied mix of shops, restaurants, and music venues, to the historic elegance of Lafayette Square with its Victorian mansions. With its variety of real eateries and stores, the

Italian-American area of The Hill provides a gastronomic adventure. One of the city's oldest neighborhoods, Soulard, is well-known for its bustling nightlife and farmers market.

Without discussing its gastronomic delights, no introduction to St. Louis would be complete. With a mouthwatering variety of flavors, the city's culinary scene is as varied as its people. The melting pot of influences in the city is reflected in local specialties like toasted ravioli, gooey butter cake, and barbecue in the St. Louis style. With a plethora of breweries and beer gardens offering a wide variety of libations to choose from, including inventive specialty beers and classic lagers, the craft beer scene is equally amazing.

This book will accompany you as you get ready to explore the heart of St. Louis, providing helpful advice, fascinating anecdotes, and vivid images of the city. St. Louis is a city that welcomes you to stay, enjoy, and create your own unique experiences—from its colorful past to its exciting present.

The Gateway City of St. Louis welcomes you. This is where your adventure starts.

Synopsis and Fast Facts

Here are some key details and a synopsis that illustrate what makes St. Louis special and fascinating so that you may quickly learn about it:

Population and Demographics

The population of St. Louis City is roughly 300,000, but that of the broader metropolitan area, sometimes known as broader St. Louis, is roughly 2.8 million. The city is renowned for its varied neighborhoods, each contributing to its lively social fabric with a unique combination of cultures.

Climatic Conditions

St. Louis is situated on the western bank of the Mississippi River in the eastern portion of Missouri. The city has a total area of roughly 66 square miles. With hot, muggy summers and chilly winters, the climate is categorized as humid subtropical. The best times to travel are in the spring and fall since they are temperate and enjoyable.

Business and Economy

St. Louis, which was once a significant port city, has a robust manufacturing, transportation, and commerce base. The biotechnology, healthcare, education, and financial services sectors are among those that the city is now a center for. Anheuser-Busch, Emerson Electric, and Monsanto are a few of the significant companies with local headquarters.

Transportation

With a large number of domestic and international flights, the main airport is St. Louis Lambert International Airport (STL).

Major attractions and communities are easily accessible through the city's Metro Transit public transportation system, which consists of buses and the MetroLink light rail system.

Major highways provide excellent access to St. Louis, making driving to and within the city simple.

Industry and Education

The location of numerous notable universities, such as Washington University in St. Louis, Saint Louis University, and the University of Missouri-St. Louis. The city is well-known for its creativity, especially in the domains of technology and health care, and it boasts a thriving startup environment.

Recreation and Sports

With professional clubs like the St. Louis Blues (NHL) and St. Louis Cardinals (MLB), St. Louis is a sports lover's dream come true.
After St. Louis City SC joined Major League Soccer in 2023, soccer fans can anticipate watching their games.
There are plenty of places to relax and have fun outside, including parks, trails, and outdoor activities.

Cultural and Historic Highlights

The city is home to a plethora of museums, galleries, theaters, and music venues, all contributing to its rich cultural landscape. The Old Courthouse, the site of the Dred Scott case, and the famous Eads Bridge, the first steel bridge to span the Mississippi River, are just two examples of St. Louis's well-preserved architectural legacy.

Festivals and Events

Throughout the year, St. Louis holds several festivals and events honoring anything from art and history to music and cuisine.
Notable occasions include the Great Forest Park Balloon Race, the St. Louis International Film Festival, and Fair St. Louis, an Independence Day celebration that attracts big audiences for its family-friendly activities, concerts, and fireworks.

Food and Drink

A combination of classic dishes and cutting-edge creations make up the vibrant and varied culinary scene.

Delicious butter cake, toasted ravioli, and St. Louis-style pizza with Provel cheese on top are among the local specialties.

With many breweries and beer gardens where guests can sip locally brewed beers, the city is home to a flourishing craft beer sector.

Neighboring Regions

St. Louis is ideally situated near numerous other significant cities, such as Kansas City, Chicago, and Indianapolis, which makes it a great starting point for additional Midwest exploration. In addition to outdoor activities in places like the Mark Twain National Forest and the Ozark Mountains, the surrounding area offers picturesque drives and quaint small towns.

St. Louis is a city of surprises and contrasts, where modern construction coexists with old sites. The Gateway City extends a warm welcome and countless opportunities to all visitors, whether they plan to stay for a little while or a long time.

Best Times to Visit

As a year-round destination, St. Louis has something exceptional to offer in every season. The ideal time to go, however, will vary depending on the kind of experience you want. This information will assist you in determining the best time to book your travel.

Springtime (March-May)

A trip to St. Louis in the spring is pleasant. The pleasant weather is ideal for outdoor activities, with temperatures ranging from the mid-50s to the mid-70s Fahrenheit. Particularly in areas like Forest Park and the Missouri Botanical Garden, the city is alive with vibrant foliage and blooming flowers.

Key Events:

- Missouri Botanical Garden's Orchid Show:
  The Orchid Show at the Missouri Botanical Garden is a breathtaking exhibition of orchids that attracts tourists from all over.

- St. Louis Earth Day Festival:

Among the biggest events in the nation, this festival offers eco-friendly merchants, live music, and educational programs.

- St. Louis Cardinals Opening Day:
Fans converge on Busch Stadium to support their favorite club as the baseball season begins.

Summer: (August through June)

In St. Louis, summertime temperatures frequently reach the upper 80s and 90s Fahrenheit, making it a warm and muggy season. It's a popular time for travelers despite the heat because there are many outdoor festivals and activities.

Main Events:

- Fair St. Louis – This enormous celebration, which takes place around July 4th, has concerts, fireworks, and family-friendly events.

- Great Forest Park Balloon Race:
A breathtaking occasion featuring vibrant hot air balloons flying to the sky.

- Music at the Muny: Experience outdoor musical theater shows at the oldest and largest outdoor theater in America, Music at the Muny.

Fall: (October through November)

Visiting St. Louis in the fall is arguably the greatest option. Comfortable temperatures, between the mid-60s to mid-70s Fahrenheit, are experienced, and the city's parks and neighborhoods are beautifully framed by the fall foliage. When the summer throngs aren't around, it's the perfect time to enjoy outdoor activities.

Main Events:

- Louis International Film Festival:
  The St. Louis International Film Festival** is a festival of films that includes special activities, workshops, and screenings.

- Taste of St. Louis:
  A culinary enthusiast's dream come true, Taste of St. Louis offers cuisine from some of the top eateries in the city.

- Oktoberfest: MLlA boisterous celebration of German culture in Soulard that includes food, drink, and live music.

Winter (December–February)

St. Louis experiences frigid winters, with regular lows in the 30s and 40s Fahrenheit and sporadic snowfall. Despite being the least busy time of year for tourists, it has a distinct charm and lots of fun events.

Noteworthy Events:

- Holiday Light Shows:
  The city comes alive with stunning displays, like the Garden Glow at the Missouri Botanical Garden and the Anheuser-Busch Brewery Lights.

- St. Louis Blues Hockey:
  Take in a nail-biting match and witness the locals' fervor for their NHL team.

- Mardi Gras in Soulard:
  One of the biggest Mardi Gras events in the nation, Mardi Gras in Soulard offers parades, live music, and colorful celebrations.

St. Louis offers a plethora of experiences, regardless of when you decide to visit. There is always something intriguing to see and do because each season brings with it its special events and atmosphere. St. Louis offers you a ton of chances for adventure and welcomes you with open arms, whether you're wandering through a park full of flowers in the spring, taking in a summer festival, admiring the fall foliage, or feeling the beauty of the winter lights.

Chapter 2

The Gateway Arch

The Gateway Arch is a magnificent monument that honors the city's crucial role in the US government's westward expansion and serves as the city's distinguishing emblem. Designed by the Finnish-American architect Eero Saarinen, this imposing monument is a striking symbol of ambition and discovery in addition to being a feat of contemporary engineering.

Historic Importance

To commemorate President Thomas Jefferson's Louisiana Purchase and the ensuing Lewis and Clark Expedition, the Jefferson National Expansion Memorial project included the concept of the Gateway Arch. In 1947, a design competition was launched to create the monument, and Eero Saarinen's modern and elegant design won. 1963 saw the start of construction, and 1965 saw its completion. With a height of 630 feet, the Arch is now the highest man-made landmark in the country.

Building and Design

Constructed from stainless steel and engineered to endure the test of time and natural forces, the Gateway Arch is a wonder of engineering. Both an artistic achievement and a structural first is its distinctive inverted catenary shape. The base of the Arch is 60 feet below the surface, offering stability and support. Constructed concurrently, each leg of the Arch rose from the earth in a carefully timed fashion until they met at the summit. The last component, a keystone, was expertly placed to finish the building.

Explorer Experience

With its breathtaking vistas and insightful look into American history, a visit to the Gateway Arch is sure to leave a lasting impression. Here's what to anticipate when you go:

Gateway Arch National Park:
In addition to the Old Courthouse and the Museum at the Gateway Arch, the Arch is a component of the broader Gateway Arch National

Park. The park itself is a gorgeously designed space with several perspectives of the Arch, ideal for strolls and picnics.

The Museum at the Gateway Arch:
This museum offers an immersive journey into the history of St. Louis and the westward development and is situated at the foot of the Arch. Engaging displays, historical relics, and interactive exhibits explain the narrative of the Native American tribes, the early settlers, and the important events that impacted the area.

The Tram Ride to the Top:
To visit the Gateway Arch is not complete without taking the thrilling tram trip to the top. The team is made up of several little pods that climb into the Arch's interior and have the form of an egg. An observation deck with glass providing expansive views of St. Louis, the Mississippi River, and the surrounding surroundings may be found once reaching the summit of the approximately four-minute ride. Up to thirty kilometers are visible in each direction on a clear day.

The Old Courthouse:
Another important monument is The Old Courthouse, which is only a short stroll from the Arch. Numerous significant trials took place there, most notably the Dred Scott case, which was a major factor in the events that preceded the Civil War. Learn more about this important period in American history by taking a tour of the reconstructed courtrooms.

Riverfront Activities:
Along the Mississippi River, there are many things to do in the vicinity of the Gateway Arch. To discover more about the history of the river and its significance to St. Louis, you may take a picturesque riverboat trip or just relax and take in the scenery from one of the numerous overlooks along the riverside.

Activities and Events

The Gateway Arch organizes several programs and activities all year long with the goal of enlightening and entertaining tourists. These consist of unique events honoring significant anniversaries in American history, instructional activities for school groups, and historical reenactments. The Arch grounds are a bustling center of activity in the city since they are frequently used for festivals, concerts, and community meetings.

A Useful Guide

Here are some useful suggestions to bear in mind while organizing your trip to the Gateway Arch:

Tickets:
If possible, get your tickets in advance for the museum and the tram trip, especially during the busiest travel times. Purchases of tickets can be made at the Gateway Arch Ticket Center or online.

Security:
The Arch requires all visitors to go through security screening to enter. Don't forget to give this procedure more time.

Accessibility:
The Gateway Arch is dedicated to ensuring accessibility. Visitors with disabilities can use the majority of the facilities, the grounds, and the museum. However, people with mobility problems could find the tram journey to the summit challenging.

Weather Considerations:
Although the Arch is always open, visibility from the top might be impacted by the weather. Make sure you consider the forecast while making plans.

The Gateway Arch is more than simply a landmark; it represents the resilience of St. Louis and the city's important place in American history. A trip to the Gateway Arch is a must for anybody visiting St. Louis, whether they are admiring its architectural magnificence, learning about the history in its museum, or just taking in the view from its observation deck. Encapsulating the spirit of the Gateway City, this renowned monument provides a profound link to the past as well as an inspirational picture of what lies ahead.

Forest Park Attractions

Many refer to Forest Park as the "heart of St. Louis." It is one of the biggest urban parks in the country, with more than 1,300 acres. It attracts both residents and visitors with its abundance of attractions and activities. Since its founding in 1876, Forest Park has hosted several noteworthy occasions, including the Summer Olympics and the World's Fair in 1904. It still serves as a vital component of the city today, offering the ideal fusion of leisure, culture, and the outdoors. This is a thorough overview of some of the park's most well-known features:

The St. Louis Zoo

Almost 17,000 creatures from almost 600 species may be found in the St. Louis Zoo, one of the top zoological parks in the nation. Through study, entertainment, and educational initiatives, the zoo aims to preserve animals and their natural environments. The best part is that everyone may visit the zoo because the entrance is free.

Highlights:
The Penguin & Puffin Coast provides a close-up look at these amazing birds, and the River's Edge is an immersive exhibit with elephants, hippos, and cheetahs. Children's Zoo and Conservation Carousel are two of the most popular attractions for them.

Special Programs:
The zoo hosts educational programs, different seasonal events, and behind-the-scenes visits. During the holidays, the zoo is transformed into a sparkling winter paradise by the Wild Lights celebration.

St Louis Art Museum

The St. Louis Art Museum is a shining example of creativity and culture, perched on Art Hill. From ancient civilizations to modern art, the museum's collection includes pieces from many eras and continents.

Exhibits:

Rembrandt, Van Gogh, Monet, and Picasso are among the well-known painters represented in the museum's permanent collection. There's always something fresh to see because of the frequent rotation of special exhibitions.

Entrance:
There is a cost for special displays; general entrance is free. Free entry days and special events draw sizable crowds and offer more chances to engage with art in novel ways.

Missouri History Museum

The history of St. Louis, Missouri, and the larger Midwest area may be explored in great detail at the Missouri History Museum.

Exhibits:
Permanent displays include the history of local sports teams, the 1904 World's Fair, and the city's role in westward development. A comprehensive look at a variety of facets of American history and culture is offered by temporary displays.

Programs:
The museum offers family-friendly events, seminars, and lectures. The museum experience is enhanced by special activities such as historical reenactments and live music performances.

Muny

America's largest and oldest outdoor musical theater is The Muny, formally known as The Municipal Theatre Association of St. Louis. With more than 11,000 seats, it provides an amazing setting for Broadway-style shows beneath the sky.

Season:
From mid-June to mid-August, The Muny presents a range of shows, from modern hits to classic musicals.

Tickets:

The Muny makes free seats available to everyone on a first-come, first-served basis, however, preferred seating necessitates the purchase of a ticket.

Saint Louis Science Center

Offering engaging exhibits and experiential learning opportunities for people of all ages, the Saint Louis Science Center is a haven for inquisitive minds.

Exhibits:
The OMNIMAX Theater, the James S. McDonnell Planetarium, and the life-size animatronic dinosaurs are among the exhibits' highlights. A wide range of interests is satisfied by the center's coverage of subjects, which includes ecology and space exploration.

Programs:
Science exhibits, workshops, and educational events are planned regularly. With a focus on the convergence of science fiction and science fact, the First Fridays event series presents films and related activities.

The Jewelry Box

Within Forest Park, there's a peaceful haven to be found in The Jewel Box, an exquisite Art Deco greenhouse and flower conservatory. It was refurbished and reopened in 2002 after being constructed in 1936.

Displays:
Tropical plants, towering palms, and lovely seasonal floral displays may all be found inside this establishment.

Events:
The Jewel Box's romantic surroundings and calm atmosphere make it a well-liked location for weddings and other special occasions.

The Boathouse

A beautiful location for dining and entertainment is the Boathouse in Forest Park. It's the perfect spot to unwind and take in the splendor of the park, situated on Post-Dispatch Lake.

Dining:
The Boathouse restaurant offers a selection of American cuisine and has both indoor and outdoor dining areas with stunning lake views.

Recreation:
Guests may hire kayaks, canoes, and paddle boats to explore the lake at their own pace.

World's Fair Pavilion

A magnificent edifice that commemorates the 1904 World's Fair is the World's Fair Pavilion. It provides a breathtaking view of the surroundings and the park.

Events:
In addition to hosting many public events, concerts, and festivals, the pavilion is accessible for private parties. It is a well-liked option for business gatherings and weddings due to its lovely outside style.

Steinberg Skating Rink

The Steinberg Skating Rink turns a portion of Forest Park into a fun place to go ice skating throughout the winter.

Experience:
The rink is the biggest outdoor skating rink in the Midwest, complete with rental skates, a campfire area, and a quaint café that serves sandwiches and hot chocolate.

Season:
The rink is a must-visit for anybody wishing to experience a classic winter pastime. It is usually open from mid-November through February.

With a wide range of attractions suitable for all ages and interests, Forest Park is a gem of St. Louis. Forest Park offers countless opportunities for leisure and exploration, regardless of your interests—history buff, art enthusiast, nature lover, or just searching for a place to unwind and have fun. Explore its delights and make lifelong memories as you explore this expansive urban sanctuary.

Cathedral Basilica of Saint Louis

The Cathedral Basilica of Saint Louis is a stunning example of both architectural grandeur and spiritual devotion, as we continue our investigation of St. Louis' prominent sites. Located in the Central West End area, this cathedral is one of the most breathtaking buildings in the city, luring tourists in with its breathtaking beauty and deep feeling of peace.

Historic Importance

Near the Mississippi River, the Old Cathedral was replaced with the Cathedral Basilica of Saint Louis, often known as the New Cathedral. 1907 saw the start of construction, and 1914 saw the dedication. With the installation of the last mosaics, the cathedral was finished in its entirety in 1988. The attention to detail and skill required to create such an amazing house of worship are evident in this timeline.

Building and Style

Romanesque and Byzantine architectural features merge to create the famous Cathedral Basilica. Green domes and ornate brickwork adorn the facade, but the inside is what grabs your attention.

Mosaics:
With more than 83,000 square feet of mosaics, the cathedral's interior is home to one of the greatest mosaic collections in the world. Artists from Italy, Germany, and the United States produced

these mosaics, which show images from the Old and New Testaments together with the history of the Catholic Church in St. Louis. An air of awe and astonishment is created by the mosaics' vivid colors and fine craftsmanship.

The Dome:
Enormous mosaics that tell the creation myth adorn the central dome, which rises 143 feet above the ground. This feature draws the attention upward and evokes awe, making it the cathedral's focal point.

Chapels and Altars:
The cathedral has several chapels, each with its layout and function. A noteworthy location for introspection is the All Souls Chapel, which is devoted to honoring the remembrance of all dead souls. Another feature that stands out is the high altar, which is constructed of marble and onyx and represents the holiness of the area.

Visitor Experience

More than just an architectural treat for the eyes, a visit to the Cathedral Basilica of Saint Louis is a soul-stirring spiritual trip.

Guided Tours:
Available tours let visitors fully understand the artistic importance and lengthy history of the cathedral. Insights into the mosaics' construction, the cathedral's architectural layout, and its historical background are offered by knowledgeable guides.

- Cathedral Basilica Tour Program:
  A suggested payment of $2 per participant is offered for daily excursions conducted by the official tour program, Cathedral Basilica Tour Program. The historical history and mosaics of the cathedral are fully examined throughout these trips.

- Private Group excursions:

You may organize private group excursions for a more customized experience. Large parties such as school groups or religious organizations might benefit greatly from these visits. Depending on the size of the party and the duration of the tour, the cost of a private tour might vary, usually between $25 and $50. It's best to make reservations in advance.

Mass and Services:
The cathedral hosts regular masses, which include daily services and special festivities, for people who would like to attend a service. Worshippers will remember this special day because of the grandeur of the venue, which heightens the spiritual experience.

Concerts and Events:
Due to its superb acoustics, the cathedral is a well-liked location for musical events like concerts. World-class performers and choirs are brought in for the Cathedral Concerts series, which features performances of sacred music ranging from classical to modern. By fusing architectural magnificence with musical brilliance, these events offer a chance to appreciate the cathedral's beauty from a new perspective.

Gift Store:
Scripture texts, novels, and mementos are available at the cathedral's gift store. Meaningful mementos that honor the cathedral's creative and spiritual legacy are easily found there.

Conservation and Repair

The Cathedral Basilica of Saint Louis requires a lot of attention to maintain. Sustained conservation endeavors guarantee that this architectural treasure will persistently motivate subsequent cohorts. To preserve the integrity of its mosaics and structure, the cathedral has undergone many restoration initiatives, which demonstrate the community's dedication to protecting its spiritual and cultural legacy.

A wonder of art and architecture, the Cathedral Basilica of Saint Louis is more than just a house of worship; it is a symbol of beauty and faith. One of St. Louis's must-see landmarks, its magnificent mosaics and calm environment provide a haven for reflection and inspiration. Experience the Cathedral Basilica's ageless elegance and profound tranquility, whether you are drawn to it by its historical significance, artistic magnificence, or spiritual significance. The cathedral continues to serve as a moving reminder of the rich spiritual and cultural legacy of the city as you travel through St. Louis.

Chapter 3

City Museum

You have never visited a museum like the City Museum in St. Louis. Inviting guests to interact, explore, and get up close and personal with the exhibits, this unique attraction defies conventional museum conceptions with its quirky combination of playground, funhouse, and architectural marvel. The 600,000-square-foot City Museum, which is housed in a former shoe factory in the Washington Avenue Loft District, is a captivating imaginary world for both kids and adults.

Founders and Goals

Bob Cassilly, an artist and businessman, had the idea for the City Museum to establish a place where play and art collide. Repurposed architectural and industrial elements from throughout the city were used in the museum's construction, which gave it a unique appeal when it opened in 1997. Deviating from the conventional "look but don't touch" museum approach, Cassilly wanted to create an environment that sparked curiosity, creativity, and discovery.

Creative Masterpiece

Every nook and cranny of the museum itself is intended to astonish and inspire, making it an architectural wonder. The structure's exposed brick, tall columns, and large open areas all reflect its industrial origins. The City Museum's unique features, such as airplane fuselages hovering in midair, enormous slides that spiral across many levels, and intricate mosaics that cover whole walls, are what set it apart.

Exhibits and Attractions

There are many displays and activities available at the City Museum, all of them being more creative than the last. Here are some of the highlights, examined in more detail:

MonstroCity:
One of the most recognizable aspects of the City Museum is MonstroCity. It's an outdoor playground made out of salvaged items like fire engines, abandoned airplanes, and cranes. With its complicated network of tunnels, bridges, and towers, this multi-level construction challenges visitors to climb, crawl, and slide. For both kids and adults, it's an exciting event that offers a special fusion of art and adventure.

Enchanted Caves and Shoe Shafts:
The Enchanted Caves and Shoe Shafts provide an underground maze of tunnels, slides, and hidden passageways. They are located deep within the museum. These shafts, which once served as a conveyor system for the shoe factory, have been turned into an underground wonderland. There are numerous story chutes, secret chambers to find, and twisting passageways for visitors to explore.

World Aquarium:
Another attraction inside the City Museum is the two-story World Aquarium, which showcases a wide range of aquatic creatures. Here, guests may witness feedings, engage with touch tanks, and discover more about marine environments. The aquarium gives the unique mix of the museum a natural touch while also adding an educational element to the excitement.

Architectural Museum:
Located on the fourth level, this museum features a collection of repurposed architectural pieces from several historic structures in St. Louis. With items ranging from elaborate wrought ironwork to magnificent cornices and columns, this show honors the city's rich architectural legacy. Highlighting the workmanship and style of bygone eras, it's an intriguing look into the past.

Art City:
This place provides a hands-on art studio where guests may be creative and work on a variety of art projects. This interactive area promotes artistic expression and exploration in a variety of mediums, including mixed media, sculpting, and painting and sketching. Families may create together here and have a one-of-a-kind souvenir of their trip.

Roof Top:
A school bus dangling perilously on the edge of the building, a gigantic slide, and a Ferris wheel are among the extra attractions available on the museum's Roof Top rooftop, which also gives stunning views of the St. Louis cityscape. A fascinating addition to the museum's inside exhibitions, the rooftop is open periodically.

Visitor Experience

A trip to the City Museum is an experience that never ends. To maximize your experience, consider the following advice:

What to Wear:
Since there will be a lot of climbing, crawling, and sliding around the museum, comfortable attire and closed-toe shoes are required. Accept the museum's lively vibe and be ready to get a bit messy.

When to Visit:
The museum may get busy, particularly on weekends and during the summer break. You may skip the busiest hours and have a more laid-back experience by coming early or going during the weekdays.

Age Considerations:
Though the City Museum is appropriate for all ages, extremely small children or individuals with mobility impairments may find some places difficult. Numerous spaces are reserved especially for younger guests, such as Toddler Town, which provides a fun and secure atmosphere for young children.

Food and Drink:

There are several places to eat in the museum, including snack bars and a café, where a wide selection of food and beverages are available. If you would rather pack your lunch, there are picnic places as well.

Safety:
While the City Museum is meant to be an exciting place, it's crucial to be mindful of your surroundings and keep a close eye on little children. Although there are many hidden corners to discover and the museum personnel are attentive to security, it's advisable to proceed with caution.

Admission and Tours

General admission tickets to the City Museum grant entry to the majority of the museum's displays and activities. The current entry costs are as follows:

General Admission:
$38 for those three years of age and up. Children under three go in for free.

Rooftop Admission:
Access to the rooftop attractions is available for an extra $8 during certain seasons.

Guided tours are offered for anyone who wants to learn more about the history and architecture of the museum. These tours offer intriguing perspectives into the development of the museum and its displays. Guided tours are extra and usually cost roughly $10 per person on top of basic entry.

The strength of imagination and ingenuity is demonstrated by the City Museum. It offers a humorous, engaging, and completely original experience that defies conventional ideas of what a museum ought to be. Experience an unforgettable trip at the City Museum, whether you want to explore the breathtaking MonstroCity, explore the Enchanted Caves, or create your masterpiece in Art City. It's a destination where art, architecture, and play all come together to create a spectacular experience that appeals to all age groups and is a must-see for anybody visiting St. Louis.

Missouri History Museum

The rich and varied history of St. Louis, Missouri, and the Midwest area as a whole are fascinatingly explored at the Missouri History Museum, which is housed in the lovely Forest Park. A combination of permanent and rotating exhibitions that showcase the social, cultural, and political history of the region are offered by the museum, which is housed in the Jefferson Memorial Building, built with funds from the 1904 World's Fair. For both history buffs and casual tourists, this institution is a must-visit since it is more than simply a storehouse of antiquities; it is a vibrant hub for learning and discovery.

Credibility in History

Established by the Missouri Historical Society in 1866, the Missouri History Museum is among the region's oldest historical establishments. A further degree of historical significance is added by its placement in Forest Park, the site of the 1904 World's Fair. The goal of the museum is to increase knowledge about historical events and how they affect the present and the future.

Building Beauty

Primarily an architectural marvel, the Jefferson Memorial Building is the main building of the museum. Enormous columns, elaborate brickwork, and a magnificent dome characterize its Classical Revival construction. Recognizing Jefferson's contribution to the Louisiana Purchase and the westward expansion, this structure served as the nation's first memorial. More exhibition space and improved visitor experiences were offered with the opening of the contemporary Emerson Center in 2000.

Permanent Exhibits

Numerous long-term displays at the Missouri History Museum offer an in-depth look at the history of the area. These include:

1904 World's Fair: Looking Back at Looking Forward":
Explore the splendor and significance of the Louisiana Purchase Exposition, popularly known as the 1904 St. Louis World's Fair. Exhibition pieces, images, and narratives that encapsulate the

inventiveness and cross-cultural interaction that typified the fair are displayed here.

"Seeking St. Louis":
This exhibit covers the whole history of St. Louis from its inception in 1764 to the present, and is divided into two sections: "Currents" and "Reflections." "Reflections" presents first-hand accounts from city dwellers, illuminating the social and cultural forces that have created St. Louis, whereas "Currents" concentrates on the city's expansion and shifting topography.

"The Louisiana Purchase":
This display delves into the importance of the 1803, double-sided United States that helped spur westward migration. Visitors learn about this significant event and its long-lasting effects on American history via maps, records, and relics.

Rotating Exhibits

A wide selection of rotating exhibits covering various themes are hosted by the Missouri History Museum in addition to its permanent displays. You may constantly see and learn something new thanks to these temporary exhibits:

Cultural Exhibits:
An exploration of the rich cultural legacy of St. Louis and Missouri is the subject of several exhibitions held at the museum. These displays provide a richer knowledge of the community's diverse cultural fabric by focusing on topics such as African American history and immigrant experiences.

Social and Political History: Changing displays also explore important social and political movements, including background information and critiques of important persons and events. Discussions have included the history of labor unions in the area, women's suffrage, and the Civil Rights Movement.

Photography and Art:

The museum frequently hosts pictures and art displays that document the area's visual heritage. A distinct viewpoint on the history and culture of the region is offered by these displays, which showcase the work of regional photographers and painters.

Educational Programs and Events

Community participation and education are the two main goals of the Missouri History Museum. To inform and motivate guests of all ages, it provides a broad range of activities and programs.

Lectures and Workshops:
The museum regularly conducts lectures and workshops on a variety of themes about Missouri and American history, with historians, writers, and other specialists leading the sessions. Encouraging a better comprehension of historical events, these workshops offer deeper insights into the displays.

Family Activities:
The museum often hosts events and programs that are appropriate for families. Younger visitors might find history interesting and approachable through interactive exhibitions, practical activities, and storytelling sessions.

Special Events:
The museum hosts a variety of year-round special events, including neighborhood festivals, holiday celebrations, and historical reenactments. These occasions give a distinctive perspective on history and a vibrant atmosphere.

Visitor Information

For people of all ages, including families and organizations, a trip to the Missouri History Museum is gratifying. For your visit planning, be aware of the following:

Entry:

The museum's general entry is free, although there can be fees for some special exhibitions and activities. Everyone is guaranteed the chance to explore and learn because of this accessibility.

Hours:
The museum is open every day, except Tuesdays, when its hours are extended. As the museum is closed on some holidays, it's a good idea to check their website for the most recent hours as well as any special dates.

Tours:
The museum provides guided tours that give a comprehensive examination of the exhibits and the historical context they depict. For school groups, organizations, and tourists looking for a more in-depth look, group excursions are a great choice and may be scheduled in advance.

- Public Tours:
  Lasting approximately one hour, these excursions are offered at no cost. The highlights of the museum are covered in these tours, which also include the key exhibitions.

- Private Group Tours: Individualized group tours may be scheduled for a more customized experience. Usually costing about $50 for parties up to 20, these trips may be customized based on the interests of the group.

Preservation and Research

A hub for research and preservation, the Missouri History Museum also serves as a venue for public education. Abundant collections of papers, photos, maps, and other historical items may be found at the museum's research center and library. With the use of these materials, scholars, students, and researchers may carry out investigations and learn more about Missouri's past.

To vividly depict the rich and varied history of St. Louis and Missouri, the Missouri History Museum is an essential institution.

The museum provides an immersive historical experience with its wide-ranging exhibits, captivating activities, and stunning location in Forest Park. The Missouri History Museum offers an invaluable and illuminating trip through time, regardless of your interests—the vast spectacle of the 1904 World's Fair, the detailed tales of the city's citizens, or the more general historical histories of the Midwest. A chance to meaningfully and enduringly engage with history is provided by this location where the past and present collide.

National Blues Museum

A lively celebration of the rich legacy and cultural relevance of blues music, the National Blues Museum is situated in the center of St. Louis' downtown. American music and culture have been greatly impacted by the blues, an art form whose heritage is being preserved and honored at this museum, which opened its doors in 2016. For fans of both music and history, the museum is a must-visit since it provides an immersive experience that explores the origins of the blues, its development, and its influence on other musical genres.

Credibility in History

The history of America is intricately intertwined with the blues. Rooted in African American spirituals, labor songs, and field hollers, the blues originated in the Mississippi Delta during the late 19th and early 20th centuries. The blues gave rise to regional blues genres in places such as Chicago, Memphis, and St. Louis as blues performers moved northward, bringing their music with them. Jazz, rock 'n' roll, R&B, and soul have all benefited greatly from blues music, as the National Blues Museum demonstrates, as well as its rich history.

Building Beauty

A magnificently renovated historic structure that combines modern and traditional design aspects is home to the National Blues

Museum. A contemporary, dynamic area intended to inspire and engage guests is found within, while the outside boasts wide windows and tasteful brickwork. The carefully considered arrangement of the museum takes visitors on a tour of the blues music's historical and thematic development, making for an engaging and instructive visit.

Permanent Exhibits

Blues music, its history, and its cultural influence are all covered in detail in the museum's permanent exhibits:

"Rivers of Rhythm Pathways":
Visitors to this interactive display may investigate the relationships between blues and other musical genres using touchscreens. Visitors may see how the blues has impacted a diverse range of musical traditions by choosing various performers, instruments, and styles.

"The Blues Hall of Fame":
This segment honors the blues music luminaries, such as Etta James, B.B. King, and Muddy Waters. Visitors are given insight into the lives and careers of these significant artists through images, biographies, and artifacts.

"Crossroads":
Tracing the blues' migration from the Mississippi Delta to American cities, this show explores the blues' historical and cultural origins. Key players who influenced the blues are highlighted, and the social and economic circumstances that gave origin to the genre are examined.

"Mix It Up":
The interactive exhibit "Mix It Up" allows visitors to use digital tools to compose original blues music. They may learn about the songwriting process and get a greater understanding of the artistry required in producing blues music by experimenting with different beats, instruments, and lyrics.

"Sweet Home Chicago":

The Chicago blues scene, one of the most significant regional blues music genres, is the subject of the exhibit "Sweet Home Chicago". It features memorabilia and anecdotes from well-known Chicago blues performers, highlighting the migration of blues musicians to Chicago and the emergence of electric blues.

Rotating Exhibits

A rotating exhibition series exploring different facets of blues music and its cultural influence is also held at the National Blues Museum. You may constantly see and learn something new thanks to these temporary exhibits:

Artist Spotlights:
These shows highlight certain blues artists and offer a comprehensive look at their lives, works, and influences on the genre. In the past, Koko Taylor and Howlin' Wolf have been highlighted musicians.

Thematic Exhibits:
Changing displays may also go into more general topics related to blues music, such as the blues' impact on popular music, women's roles in the genre, or the connection between blues and social movements.

Educational Programs and Events

To inform and inspire visitors of all ages, the National Blues Museum is dedicated to community involvement and education. To this end, it offers a range of activities and events.

Workshops and Classes:
A variety of topics related to blues music are covered in these workshops and classes, ranging from its cultural relevance and historical background to applied music theory. Offering practical learning experiences, these programs cater to a wide range of ability levels.

Live Events:

Local and national blues musicians frequently play live at the museum. Visitors get the chance to feel the intensity and passion of blues music in a small-scale setting at these performances.

Family Activities:
The museum often hosts events and programs that are appropriate for families. Blues music is made approachable and interesting for younger audiences through interactive exhibitions, interactive workshops, and storytelling sessions.

Special Events:
In addition to regular film screenings and lecture series, the museum hosts blues festivals and other special events all year long. In addition to offering distinctive opportunities to enjoy and explore blues music, these events foster a dynamic atmosphere.

Visitor Information

Groups, families, and individuals may all benefit from a visit to the National Blues Museum. For your visit planning, be aware of the following:

Entry:
To access the museum, general admission tickets are needed. Currently, the following are the entrance fees:

- Adults: $15
- Seniors (65 and over): $12
- Students (with ID): $10
- Children (5–12): $5
- Children under 5: free

Hours:
Tuesday through Sunday are the museum's regular business hours; on weekends, these hours are extended. It is wise to check the museum's website for current hours and any special closures as it is closed on Mondays and other holidays.

Tours:
The museum provides guided tours that give a comprehensive examination of the exhibits and the historical context they depict. For school groups, organizations, and tourists looking for a more in-depth look, group excursions are a great choice and may be scheduled in advance.

- Public Tours:
 Lasting approximately one hour, these excursions are offered at no cost. The highlights of the museum are covered in these tours, which also include the key exhibitions.

- Private Group Tours:
 Individualized group tours may be scheduled for a more customized experience. For parties up to 20, these trips usually cost about $100 and may be tailored to the interests of the party.

Store and Gift Shop

Gifts, clothing, souvenirs, vinyl records, CDs, books, and other blues-related items are all available in the museum's gift store. For a buddy who enjoys music, it's the ideal spot to locate a keepsake from your trip.

The museum's café offers a comfortable place to unwind and consider your visit if you're only stopping by for a snack or a beverage. During your museum tour, the menu is a handy place to stop and enjoy a variety of snacks, sandwiches, and beverages.

A vivid monument to the long tradition of blues music is the National Blues Museum. The museum presents a thorough and engrossing examination of the blues and its significant influence on American society through its immersive displays, intriguing programming, and exciting events. A stimulating experience that honors the blues' legacy, creativity, and passion is offered by the National Blues Museum, regardless of your level of familiarity with the music. Visitors are invited to connect with history and recognize the enduring power of the blues at this place where music history is brought to life.

Anheuser-Busch Brewery Tour

Without seeing the renowned Anheuser-Busch Brewery, a vacation to St. Louis would not be complete. In addition to combining history, culture, and of course, the craft of beer making, this historic location provides an immersive experience. The Anheuser-Busch Brewery, one of the biggest and oldest breweries in the country, is situated in the Soulard area. An interesting look at the company's history, the brewing process, and the legacy of its most well-known product, Budweiser, may be had by taking a tour of the brewery.

Historic Importance

Established in 1852 by German immigrants, Adolphus Busch and Eberhard Anheuser, the Anheuser-Busch Brewery has been instrumental in shaping the course of American brewing history. Pasteurization and the use of chilled railcars were two of the company's breakthroughs that completely changed the beer market. These developments set the stage for Anheuser-Busch's success and assisted in making the company a household name. The brewery still stands as a tribute to the inventiveness and spirit of enterprise of its founders today.

Architectural Magnificence

Modern and traditional structures coexist in the Anheuser-Busch Brewery complex. Some of the red brick buildings are from the 19th century, and they have elaborate facades and exquisite architectural elements. One of the highlights of the visit is the brew house, with its imposing copper kettles and windows made of stained glass. The brewery is an interesting location to explore since it combines aesthetic beauty with industrial functionality.

Experiencing a Brewery Tour

The Anheuser-Busch Brewery Tour provides a thorough examination of the whole brewing process, from the choice of ingredients to the final product's packaging. With several opportunities to sample beer and observe the brewing process up close, the tour is meant to be both entertaining and instructive.

Highlights of the tour:

Clydesdale Stables:
The tour starts with a visit to the historic stables where the world-famous Budweiser Clydesdales are kept. Since 1933, these magnificent horses have represented Anheuser-Busch. Guests may take pictures with this kind of giant and learn about their upkeep and training.

Brew House:
The Brew House is the center of the brewery and the place where magic is made. Visitors may discover the components and methods used to make Budweiser as well as view the enormous copper kettles used to brew the beer. This contemporary facility is given a historical flavor by the elaborate stained glass windows and antique brewing apparatus.

Fermentation Cellars:
The trip proceeds to the fermentation cellars, where the critical fermentation process is applied to the beer. In addition to learning about the chemistry of fermentation and maturing, guests can view the big tanks where the beer is kept.

Packaging Plant:
Anheuser-Busch's activities are demonstrated by this impressive example of modern technology, which also shows off the company's size and efficiency. The filling, capping, and distribution of bottles and cans are visible to visitors. The packing process's remarkable speed and accuracy offer light on how the brewery fulfills the strong demand for its goods.

Historic Brewhouse:
From the late 19th century, the wonderfully maintained historic brewhouse is one of the tour's highlights. This portion of the tour explores Anheuser-Busch's past and the development of its brewing methods. Viewers may view antique brewing apparatus and discover the company's innovative and quality-controlling initiatives.

Beer Tasting:
The Anheuser-Busch Brewery Tour offers a delicious beer tasting, which is a must-have for every brewery tour. Visitors are welcome to taste a selection of Anheuser-Busch products, such as Budweiser, Bud Light, and a few specialty brews, after the tour. Visitors may enjoy the variety of tastes and beer styles that the brewery produces by partaking in the tasting experience.

Guided Tour Options

To accommodate a variety of interests and schedules, the Anheuser-Busch Brewery provides many guided tour alternatives. Every tour offers a different viewpoint on the brewing procedure and the brewery's past:

Day Fresh Tour:
The 45-minute Day Fresh Tour is ideal for anyone seeking a brief but educational encounter. In addition to covering the main points of the brewing process, it involves a tour of the Clydesdale stables and a taste of Budweiser directly from the finishing tank. Each person must pay about $10.

Brewmaster Tour:
The Brewmaster Tour provides a 2-hour tour of the brewery for those seeking a deeper experience. This tour gives you access to places like the Finishing Cellar and the Beechwood Aging Cellars that aren't on the regular tour. In addition, participants get a taste of a seasonal or limited-edition beer and a commemorative glass. The price per person is about $35.

Beer School:

For those who like to learn more about the science and art of brewing, there is **Beer School**, an ideal interactive experience. Topics including beer types, brewing methods, and food pairings are covered in the hour-long lesson. Along with a complimentary sample of many Anheuser-Busch products, participants also earn a diploma. Each person must pay about $20.

The Historic Anheuser-Busch Tour:
This tour focuses on the company's legacy and the brewery's lengthy history. It involves trips to the museum, the Clydesdale stables, and the old brewhouse. Participants gain knowledge of the innovations and contributions made by the firm to the beer sector. The price per person is about $15.

A Guide for Visitors

With the following knowledge, organizing a trip to the Anheuser-Busch Brewery is simple:

Location:
1200 Lynch Street, St. Louis, MO 63118 is the address where the brewery is situated. It has plenty of parking for guests and is conveniently accessible by vehicle.

Hours:
There are tours available every day; the first tour usually leaves at 10:00 AM and the final trip leaves at 4:00 PM. For the most up-to-date tour schedule, visit the brewery website and reserve your tickets ahead of time, especially during the busiest travel seasons.

Accessibility:
All guests will receive an accessible experience from the brewery. Wheelchair users can use the tour paths, and anyone with mobility issues can get help.

Beer Garden and Gift Shop

Following the tour, guests are welcome to purchase a range of Anheuser-Busch items from the gift store, including clothing, glasses, and memorabilia. The store has a variety of goods that would make excellent presents or mementos for beer lovers.

The brewery's beer garden is the ideal place for folks to unwind and sip on a nice beer. A menu of light meals and snacks is available, along with a variety of Anheuser-Busch beers on tap. A comfortable and relaxed setting to relax and think back on the journey is offered by the beer garden.

A remarkable fusion of culture, history, and artistry is found on the Anheuser-Busch Brewery Tour. Visitors will get the rare chance to observe up close one of the most recognizable breweries in America and discover the complex process involved in making beer. The tour offers a thorough look at Anheuser-Busch's heritage and creativity, from the state-of-the-art packaging factory to the beautiful Clydesdales. An exciting and unforgettable experience is guaranteed with the Anheuser-Busch Brewery Tour, regardless of your level of beer expertise or level of curiosity in the brewing process.

Chapter 4

St. Louis Zoo

The St. Louis Zoo, one of the best zoological parks in the country, is tucked away in the center of Forest Park. The St. Louis Zoo provides enjoyable experiences for guests of all ages and is well-known for its vast animal collection, creative displays, and dedication to wildlife protection. The zoo was established in 1910 and has expanded to cover more than 90 acres. It is now home to approximately 16,000 animals from almost 600 different species. The best part is that general entry is free, making it an inexpensive and accessible family vacation.

Historic Importance

The history of the city's public school system and community enrichment initiatives is closely linked to that of the St. Louis Zoo. The 1904 World's Fair's bird display served as the impetus for local politicians to create a permanent zoo, and so the zoo had its start. The St. Louis Zoo has constructed state-of-the-art exhibits, grown its facilities over the years, and established itself as a pioneer in the protection and care of animals.

Architectural Magnificence

The zoo offers a picturesque and tranquil setting that blends perfectly with Forest Park's natural surroundings. Wander through gorgeously designed gardens, over attractive bridges, and meander along meandering walkways. A hint of historical beauty is added to the zoo by the magnificent neoclassical architecture of the Elephant House and the famous Spanish Revival Bird House.

Exhibits and Attractions

There are many zones inside the St. Louis Zoo, each with its special exhibits and activities that highlight a wide variety of animals from throughout the globe. The following are a few standouts:

River's Edge:
Featuring animals in lifelike settings, this immersive display transports viewers across four continents. Elephants, hippos, and Andean bears are among the attractions. With an emphasis on education and conservation, the exhibit's design informs visitors about the difficulties faced by animals and the initiatives taken to preserve them.

Red Rocks:
Home to some of the zoo's most recognizable creatures, Red Rocks is home to giraffes, large cats, and hoofed creatures. In settings that replicate their natural habitats, visitors may observe lions, tigers, zebras, and other animals in the outdoor exhibitions.

The Wild:
Sea Lion Sound, Polar Bear Point, and Penguin & Puffin Coast are just a few of the well-liked displays in this area. Guests may view polar bears in a large, active environment, marvel at the amusing antics of sea lions, and watch penguins dive and swim.

Discovery Corner:
This area is ideal for younger guests as it provides opportunities for interactive learning and up-close animal interactions. This part houses the Children's Zoo, which has engaging and inspiring educational activities for kids as well as interactive exhibits and a petting area.

Historic Hill:
The Bird House, Primate House, and Herpetarium are located in this section of the zoo. Birds, primates, reptiles, and amphibians of many kinds are visible to visitors. This area of the zoo is charming because of its verdant surroundings and old-world buildings.

Lakeside Crossing:
The popular Emerson Children's Zoo, food options, and gift stores can all be found at Lakeside Crossing, which is located in the center of the zoo. It's a terrific spot for kids to explore interactive exhibits, get lunch, and take a rest.

Conservation and Education

Well known for its dedication to both teaching and conservation is the St. Louis Zoo. The zoo supports international conservation efforts, engages in several endangered species breeding projects, and carries out essential research to improve animal care and welfare. A key component of the zoo's goal is its educational programs, which provide a variety of experiences for guests of all ages.

Zoo Classes and Camps:
There are several educational programs available at the zoo, including summer camps, school field trips, and family workshops. These courses offer practical learning opportunities and promote a greater comprehension of conservation and wildlife.

Animal Encounters and Keeper Chats:
Throughout the day, zookeepers provide talks and exhibits that shed light on the habits, food, and daily care regimens of the animals. During these Q&A sessions, guests may hear directly from the experts and pose questions.

Conservation Programs:
The zoo funds several global conservation initiatives that prioritize habitat preservation, species reintroduction, and public education. Visitors may discover more about these initiatives and how they can support the preservation of wildlife.

A Guide for Visitors

With the following knowledge, organizing a trip to the St. Louis Zoo is simple:

Entrance:
Although certain exhibits and events may have a fee, general zoo entrance is free. Families can now afford to visit the zoo thanks to this approach.

Opening Times:
The zoo is open every day from 9:00 AM to 5:00 PM. The zoo's website should be checked for the most up-to-date information as hours might change depending on the season.

Parking:
A charge is required to park in the zoo's north and south lots. Additional parking may be available in adjacent Forest Park areas during peak hours. Convenient ways to get to the zoo include public transportation and shuttle services.

Dining and Shopping

The zoo has a range of food alternatives, including snack stalls and informal cafés. The Lakeside Café offers a varied cuisine with both indoor and outdoor space for guests to enjoy while dining. There are various food stalls serving snacks, beverages, and sweets around the zoo, perfect for a quick bite. Toys, clothes, and souvenirs are among the items available in the zoo's gift stores. Making purchases from these stores helps fund the zoo's conservation and educational initiatives.

Special Events and Programs

Every year, the St. Louis Zoo offers a ton of interesting special activities and events that make every visit distinctive and unforgettable:

Boo at the Zoo:
A Halloween celebration with trick-or-treating, eerie décor, and kid-focused activities. A joyful and jovial approach to commemorate the season.

Wild Lights:
With stunning light displays, Christmas-themed activities, and seasonal food, the zoo is transformed into a wintry paradise during the holiday season. For guests of all ages, it's a fantastic experience.

Family Fun Days:
Entertainment, crafts, and themed activities are all planned with families in mind. They provide you with more chances to have fun and study.

Accessibility

All visitors will have an inclusive experience from the St. Louis Zoo. Wheelchairs and strollers are available for hire, and the zoo is handicapped accessible. To further guarantee that visitors with sensory sensitivity have a pleasant experience, the zoo provides sensory-friendly materials and services.

A wealth of exciting, educational, and family-friendly activities can be found at the St. Louis Zoo. The zoo provides an engaging experience that enthralls visitors of all ages with its wide variety of animals, exquisitely crafted exhibits, and dedication to conservation. The St. Louis Zoo offers an abundance of options for enjoyment and exploration, whether you're taking in a sea lion display, stroking a goat, or learning about endangered animals. This location offers families the chance to have enduring experiences and develop a greater understanding of nature.

The Magic House

Families traveling through the city enjoy visiting The Magic House and the St. Louis Children's Museum. Children of all ages are expected to be inspired by this interactive museum to be curious, creative, and to love learning. Situated in a quaint Victorian home in Kirkwood, Missouri, The Magic House has more than 100 exhibits and interactive activities to stimulate young minds and promote inquiry via hands-on learning. The Magic House is a place where kids may play imaginatively and learn about the wonders of the world around them because of its whimsical ambiance and wide variety of displays.

Historic Importance

Two ladies from St. Louis, Jody Newman and Barbie Freund, started The Magic House in 1979 because they saw a need for a place where kids could learn by play. To accommodate additional exhibits and visitors, the museum has since undergone many expansions, growing to become a beloved institution in the St. Louis region. Today, The Magic House welcomes more than 600,000 visitors a year and inspires countless students with its cutting-edge approach to teaching.

Architectural Magnificence

The Magic House is a unique blend of a contemporary children's museum with the style and energy of a historic home. The museum's displays have a wonderful backdrop provided by the Victorian building, which makes for a special and welcoming atmosphere. Vibrant, interactive exhibits and whimsical design features abound inside the museum, capturing visitors' attention and urging investigation.

Exhibits and Attractions

From science and technology to art and culture, The Magic House offers a vast selection of exhibitions covering a wide range of themes. The following are a few standouts:

Wonderworks:
This section of the museum is intended for the youngest visitors, providing a secure and engaging setting for young children. It has several sensory play spaces, construction blocks, and activities to assist young children improve their motor skills and creativity.

Star-Spangled Center:
Children may take the oath of office, learn about the political process via interactive activities, and tour a model of the Oval Office in this patriotic display. It's a fun approach to impart civic and governmental concepts to children.

Jack and the Beanstalk Climber:
A popular attraction for younger guests is the high Jack and the Beanstalk Climber. Kids may scale the beanstalk to reach the summit, where they can navigate a variety of platforms and challenges and get an S-eye perspective of the museum.

The Children's Village:
A market, bank, library, and other community structures may be found in The Children's Village, a little village. Youngsters may practice social skills in an engaging and entertaining environment while role-playing various vocations and learning about community life.

Future Play:
With an emphasis on STEM (science, technology, engineering, and math), this exhibit invites children to explore a variety of STEM ideas via practical exercises. Future Play makes learning enjoyable and approachable, from constructing buildings with enormous blocks to investigating the fundamentals of engineering and physics.

Music Play:
Using a variety of instruments and sound experiments, kids may investigate the realm of music in this interactive display. In addition to learning about many musical genres and the physics of sound, they may compose their music.

Art Studio:
Children may let their imaginations run wild and express themselves via a variety of artistic endeavors in this place. Young artists are never short of inspiration because of the constantly evolving materials and activities available.

Make-It Workshop:
The Make-It Workshop is a maker space where kids are encouraged to work on practical building and crafts projects. They may learn about the fundamentals of engineering and design while making their creations using actual tools.

Educational Programs

Providing top-notch educational experiences that improve kids' learning and development is the Magic House's mission. The museum provides a range of activities for kids, families, and teachers.

School Field Trips:
Programs for field trips offered by The Magic House comply with both federal and state education requirements. In addition to classroom education, these programs give students practical learning opportunities.

Family Nights:
On designated family nights, parents and kids may engage in themed activities and exhibition exploration. Families may learn and connect via these activities.

Workshops and Classes:
The Magic House provides a variety of science, art, and technology-related workshops and classes. These courses offer possibilities for in-depth learning and cultivate a passion for exploration.

Outreach Programs:
The museum offers educational experiences to local groups and schools through its outreach programs, making sure that every kid may benefit from experiential learning.

Visitor Information

Organizing a trip to The Magic House is simple when you know these things:

Entry:
Groups, elderly citizens, and active military members can receive reductions off the reasonable general entrance fees. There are days when the museum provides discounted entrance prices as well.

Hours:
Open every day, the Magic House has extended hours on weekends and public holidays. To find out the most recent hours of operation as well as any special events or closures, it's a good idea to visit the museum's website.

Parking:
The museum's lot offers free parking. Public transportation is another way to get to the museum.

Dining and Shopping

Within The Magic House, the Picnic Basket Café serves a selection of kid-friendly and healthful food options, such as salads, sandwiches, and snacks. Before moving on to the exhibitions, this is the ideal place to stop and refuel. The museum's gift shop offers a range of educational toys, books, and mementos that correspond with the exhibition topics, enabling guests to carry on the educational process back home.

Special Events and Programs

Every year, The Magic House organizes a range of special events that add character and uniqueness to each visit:

Magic House Camp-Ins:
These overnight gatherings provide families and groups the chance to spend the night at the museum, where they may take advantage of unique activities, sleeping experiences in a fun and safe atmosphere, and exclusive access to the exhibits.

Holiday Celebrations:
The museum holds special events with themed crafts, activities, and entertainment for holidays including Halloween, Christmas, and Easter.

Birthday Parties:
Private party spaces, themed activities, and museum entrances are all included in the birthday party packages that The Magic House provides. It's a wonderful way to commemorate a child's birthday in a wonderful environment.

Accessibility

All guests will have an inclusive experience at The Magic House. Wheelchair accessibility and sensory-friendly amenities are offered by the museum to make sure that visitors with varying degrees of sensitivity have a pleasant experience. Special activities for families and children with impairments are also available at the museum.

Children may let their imaginations run wild, explore novel concepts, and participate in experiential learning at The Magic House. The museum offers an engaging experience that excites and inspires visitors of all ages with its varied exhibits, educational activities, and friendly ambiance. The Magic House provides countless chances for enjoyment and discovery, whether kids are climbing the beanstalk, investigating scientific concepts, or making their artwork. Families looking for an exciting and educational day in St. Louis should check it out.

Saint Louis Science Center

As we continue our investigation into family-friendly activities in St. Louis, the Saint Louis Science Center emerges as a top choice for people who are keen to learn about the wonders of technology and science. For guests of all ages, the Science Center in Forest Park provides an exciting and captivating experience. The Saint Louis Science Center encourages curiosity and a love of learning in a fun and engaging atmosphere with its wide variety of exhibits, interactive displays, and educational events.

Historic Importance

Originally run by the Saint Louis Museum of Science and Natural History, the Saint Louis Science Center started as a little planetarium in 1963. It has seen exponential growth throughout time, developing into a complete scientific museum. Adding a main building and a pedestrian bridge to the James S. McDonnell Planetarium in 1991, the scientific Center grew to become one of the biggest scientific centers in the country.

Architectural Magnificence

Modern design and useful areas that encourage investigation are combined in the Saint Louis Science Center's architecture. The sleek, modern structures are made to hold large exhibitions in a visually pleasant environment. With its recognizable dome, the planetarium is a landmark in itself and a symbol of the center's emphasis on astronomy and space.

Exhibits and Attractions

The Science Center has a vast array of displays covering a variety of scientific fields, including engineering, biology, and environmental science in addition to space research. Here are some of the main draws:

Planetarium:
Utilizing immersive presentations and breathtaking star displays, the James S. McDonnell Planetarium allows guests to learn about the universe. Viewers are taken to far-off galaxies, planetary surfaces, and beyond by the planetarium's cutting-edge projection equipment, which produces an amazing experience.

Life Science Lab:
Authentic scientific experiments and activities are conducted by guests in this interactive display. The Life Science Lab offers an amazing window into the world of biology, from studying DNA and genetics to looking at microscopic creatures.

GROW:
This one-of-a-kind display delves into the science of farming and food production. The path taken by food from farm to table, soil science, and farming methods are all available for visitors to learn about. Grow is a fun and instructive experience thanks to its interactive exhibits and outdoor garden spaces.

Ecology and Environment:
The Science Center's environmental science and sustainability area is its main emphasis. Through interactive displays, visitors may learn about conservation initiatives, ecosystems, and the effects of human activity on the environment. It's a thought-provoking place that invites guests to reflect on their environmental protection responsibilities.

Mission: Mars:
This exhibit takes visitors on an exciting expedition to the planet Mars. Through interactive exhibits, virtual reality experiences, and informative materials on the most recent developments in space research, visitors may investigate the difficulties and opportunities associated with Mars exploration.

Energy Stage:
Full of science displays and live demonstrations covering everything from chemistry and physics to engineering and technology, the Energy Stage is a must-see. For viewers of all ages, these performances offer unforgettable learning opportunities in addition to being enjoyable.

Omnimax Theater:
This theater provides an immersive movie experience thanks to its enormous dome screen. Visitors may enjoy breathtaking movies and

documentaries that highlight the marvels of space travel, science advancements, and the natural environment. An unmatched viewing experience is produced by the theater's surround sound system and high-definition projection.

Educational Programs

The Saint Louis Science Center is committed to giving guests inspiring and enlightening educational experiences. The center provides a range of educational, family, and student programs, including:

School Field Trips:
By academic requirements, the Science Center provides field trip programs that give experiential learning opportunities. These initiatives aim to raise students' interest in science and improve education in the classroom.

Science Camps:
The Science Center provides summer and school holiday camps that let kids delve deeply into particular scientific subjects. Kids may perform experiments, work on projects, and expand their scientific knowledge in an immersive learning environment offered by these programs.

Workshops and Classes:
A variety of workshops and classes catering to various age groups are held at the facility. These courses provide learners with in-depth investigation of scientific principles together with practical learning experiences covering a variety of scientific areas.

Outreach Programs:
By bringing science education to local groups and schools, The Science Center makes sure that every kid may benefit from engaging in practical scientific learning.

A Guide for Visitors

Organizing a trip to the Saint Louis Science Center is simple when you have the following information:

Entry:
The Science Center's general entry is free, although there may be fees for certain activities and displays, such as the Omnimax Theater and special exhibitions. For families, this means that the Science Center is both accessible and reasonably priced.

Opening Times:
The Science Center is open every day from 9:30 AM to 4:30 PM. For the most recent information, it's a good idea to visit the center's website as hours may change depending on the season and during special events.

Parking:
There is ample, pay parking accessible in the Science Center's lot. There are handy bus stops close by for those who wish to use public transit to get to the center.

Dining and Shopping

There are several food alternatives available at the Science Center, such as snack stalls and a café. While taking a break from perusing the exhibitions, visitors can have a meal or a short snack. The gift store of the Science Center offers a range of instructive toys, books, and mementos that correspond with the exhibition themes, enabling guests to bring a little piece of the science experience home with them.

Special Events and Programs

Every visit to the Saint Louis Science Center is distinctive and unforgettable due to the wide range of special events and activities the center offers throughout the year:

First Fridays:

The Science Center is open late on the first Friday of every month, with unique lectures, themed activities, and exhibit access. These gatherings frequently feature film screenings, keynote addresses, and interactive activities around the subject.

Science Spooktacular:
A costume contest, themed games, and eerie science presentations are all part of this Halloween celebration. Spending the holiday with the whole family is instructive and entertaining.

SciFest:
Every year, scientists, educators, and enthusiasts come together for this scientific festival to enjoy a weekend filled with interesting talks, interactive displays, and interactive activities. SciFest offers learning and exploration opportunities while celebrating the glories of science.

Accessibility

All visitors to the Saint Louis Science Center will receive an inclusive experience, we promise. To provide visitors with sensory sensitivity a comfortable visit, the center offers wheelchair accessibility as well as sensory-friendly resources and services. For guests with impairments, the Science Center also provides unique programs and accommodations.

The Saint Louis Science Center is a shining example of education and exploration, providing a wide range of engaging events and displays for kids and adults alike. The Science Center offers countless chances for education and inspiration, whether you're doing experiments in the Life Science Lab, studying the wonders of the cosmos in the planetarium, or marveling at the immersive films in the Omnimax Theater. Families may study together, pique each other's interests, and develop a deeper appreciation for the marvels of science and technology here. A trip to the Saint Louis Science Center is an exploration and learning experience rather than simply a simple tour.

Chapter 5

The Delmar Loop

The Delmar Loop is a district in St. Louis that is well worth seeing while visiting. This lively, diverse neighborhood has enough to offer everyone in terms of culture, food, entertainment, and history. Known simply as "The Loop," this Delmar Boulevard section has developed into a popular tourist destination that attracts both locals and visitors throughout time. Let's examine in detail what makes St. Louis' The Delmar Loop so worthwhile.

Historic Importance

Beginning in the early 1900s, the Delmar Loop has a long and colorful history. The former streetcar line that passed through the area's "loop," or turnaround, gave rise to the name. This area has gone through several stages of development: it was once a thriving business sector, but it also saw a period of collapse before seeing an incredible comeback spurred on by imaginative businesspeople and community activities. These days, The Loop is praised for its exceptional fusion of contemporary energy and historical beauty.

Architectural Magnificence

The architecture of The Delmar Loop is an intriguing blend of modern and old constructions. Delmar Boulevard features gorgeously restored early 20th-century facades that are home to hip stores, eateries, and entertainment centers. The area is charming and visually exciting to explore because of the contrast between the ancient and the new.

Main Draws and Highlights

Numerous landmarks and attractions that appeal to a wide range of interests may be found on the Delmar Loop:

The Pageant:
One of the most famous concert halls in St. Louis, The Pageant is a premier venue that presents a variety of shows, including comedy, drama, and rock and hip-hop. It is a favorite of both musicians and spectators due to its cozy atmosphere and superb acoustics.

Blueberry Hill:
One of the mainstays of The Loop is this iconic eatery and nightclub. In addition to its huge collection of artifacts and mouth watering cuisine, Blueberry Hill is well-known for its live music scene. Several well-known performers have graced the basement's Duck Room, including Chuck Berry, who gave frequent concerts there until his death.

Tivoli Theatre:
One of The Loop's hidden gems, this ancient theater has been exquisitely renovated. Offering a distinct cinematic experience in a refined atmosphere, it features a selection of indie films, classic films, and special screenings.

Delmar Hall:
This medium-sized concert hall provides a cozy setting for live music events. Music enthusiasts frequent this place because of its great acoustics and varied musician roster.

The Loop Trolley:
Linking Forest Park and The Loop, the Loop Trolley is a vintage streetcar line that travels down Delmar Boulevard and lends a nostalgic touch. Taking a trolley ride is an enjoyable way to explore the area and its environs while discovering its past.

Saint Louis Walk of Fame:

Stars on the sidewalks recognizing prominent figures who have contributed to St. Louis's cultural legacy may be seen as you travel down Delmar Boulevard. Celebrating writers, actresses, musicians, and other noteworthy people with connections to the city, the St. Louis Walk of Fame honors them.

Dining and Shopping

With a wide variety of eating options that capture the varied flavors of the area, the Delmar Loop is a food lover's dream come true. The Loop provides something to please every palate, whether you're in the mood for comfort food, gourmet delicacies, or foreign cuisine:

Mission Taco Joint:
Mexican-inspired street cuisine and inventive tacos are served at this well-liked location. It's a terrific spot for a casual dinner because of its inventive food and energetic environment.

Pi Pizzeria:
Acclaimed for its thin crust and deep-dish pizzas, Pi Pizzeria is a residents' and tourists' favorite. A wonderful eating experience is created by their use of premium, fresh foods.

Ranoush:
This restaurant serves real Middle Eastern food and is well-known for its tasty shawarma, falafel, and assortment of mezes. It's ideal for a casual dinner because of the cozy, welcoming ambiance.

Fitz's Root Beer:
A trip to The Loop wouldn't be complete without a stop at Fitz's, a neighborhood landmark well-known for its root beer floats and artisan sodas. The restaurant is popular with families since it also provides traditional American cuisine.

Salt + Smoke:
This is the place to go if you want a taste of barbecue in the St. Louis manner. A delightful supper is provided by their smoked meats, flavorful sides, and an assortment of specialty brews.

The Loop is home to a variety of distinctive stores and boutiques in addition to its delicious food:

Vintage Vinyl:
A sanctuary for record collectors, Vintage Vinyl has a vast assortment of new and old CDs, LPs, and memorabilia. It's a terrific location to find vintage records and hard-to-locate records.

Subterranean Books:
This independent bookshop offers a carefully chosen array of both new and secondhand books, encompassing children's books, nonfiction, and literary works. The warm, welcoming ambiance makes it the ideal place to peruse and discover your next fantastic book.

Avalon Exchange:
A chic consignment store that provides a selection of fashionable, used apparel and accessories. Fashion-forward customers searching for one-of-a-kind things frequently visit this place.

Rocket Fizz:
A nostalgic trip down memory lane may be had at **Rocket Fizz**, a quirky candy and soda business. All ages will enjoy Rocket Fizz's large assortment of candies, novelty goods, and more than 500 different types of soda.

Culture & Arts

Gallery spaces, performance venues, and public artworks are all part of the vibrant arts scene of the Delmar Loop, which is a hub for culture:

Regional Arts Commission (RAC):
A rotating exhibition of local and regional artists' work is held in the RAC Gallery. It's a fantastic location to learn about modern art and show support for St. Louis' thriving artistic community.

The Loop Arts Fest:

This yearly occasion honors the arts with interactive activities, dance performances, live music, and art displays. The Loop Arts Fest is a vibrant, kid-friendly event that showcases the creative energy of the community.

Public Art:
The Loop is home to a variety of public art projects, including sculptures, murals, and distinctive architectural elements. Visitors may enjoy a visual feast from these artworks, which also contribute to the varied character of the area.

Nightlife and Entertainment

The Delmar Loop comes alive at night with a bustling entertainment scene:

The Pageant and Delmar Hall:
Local musicians and major touring groups alike may be found performing live in these spaces. Experience concerts that will never be forgotten because of the cozy surroundings and superb acoustics.

Blueberry Hill:
Famous for its cuisine and memorabilia collection, Blueberry Hill also hosts live entertainment events, such as the iconic Duck Room.

Three Kings Public House:
A vibrant bar with a wonderful assortment of artisan beers, drinks, and delectable cuisine. It's a well-liked location for a night out because of its laid-back attitude.

Rooftop Bar at Moonrise Hotel:
Visit the rooftop bar at the Moonrise Hotel for breathtaking views of The Loop and the St. Louis skyline. This fashionable location is ideal for a laid-back evening of mingling and relaxation since it serves inventive drinks in an elegant setting.

Community and Events

The Delmar Loop is a neighborhood that offers a range of annual events and activities, not merely a destination:

Loop Ice Carnival:
A fun-filled winter event with ice sculptures, live entertainment, and family-friendly activities, the Loop Ice Carnival takes place in January. It's a special occasion that unites the neighborhood during the winter.

Indie Bookstore Day:
Honoring indie booksellers, this occasion features exclusive deals, author appearances, and literary pursuits. It's a fantastic chance to learn about new books and assist neighborhood businesses.

Small Business Saturday:
This Saturday after Thanksgiving event promotes patronage of small, neighborhood businesses by shoppers. The Loop's distinctive stores and boutiques take part in exclusive events and promotions.

An example of St. Louis's dynamic and multifaceted character is found in the Delmar Loop. The Loop provides guests with a singular and unforgettable experience thanks to its rich history, varied mix of restaurants and shopping, vibrant cultural scene, and exciting nightlife. The Delmar Loop welcomes you to immerse yourself in its dynamic energy and discover the many facets of this beloved neighborhood, whether you're enjoying a live concert at The Pageant, dining at one of the many fantastic restaurants, or just strolling along Delmar Boulevard taking in the sights.

Soulard and the Farmers Market

Soulard, one of the oldest and most historic neighborhoods in the city, is tucked away just south of the downtown area of St. Louis. The architecture and street names of this quaint neighborhood reflect its strong French ancestry. Soulard, a French surveyor who bought the site in the late 1700s, was the inspiration behind the name of the 18th-century establishment. Cobblestone streets, beautifully restored 19th-century buildings, and a lively sense of community all bear witness to the neighborhood's rich past.

Beauties of Architecture

Beautiful red-brick townhouses, wrought-iron balconies, and verdant courtyards are features of Soulard's architecture, which is an enthralling fusion of French and American styles. The neighborhood's old buildings provide a magnificent background to everyday life, giving one the impression that they are walking back in time. Soulard's remarkable architecture is a distinguishing characteristic that attracts tourists who value the fusion of urban living with old-world beauty.

Main Draws and Highlights

Farmer's Market on Sold

The famous Soulard Farmers Market, one of the country's oldest public marketplaces, is located in the center of the neighborhood. With its founding in 1779, this thriving marketplace has played a significant role in the community for more than 200 years. Fresh fruit, meats, seafood, baked goods, spices, and artisanal products are all available at this year-round market. The Soulard Farmers Market is a popular site for both locals and visitors because of its vibrant ambiance and wide assortment of items.

Produce and Fresh Goods:
Vendors in the market provide a broad selection of seasonal fruits and vegetables that are supplied from nearby farms and suppliers. Foodies will find great pleasure in the eye-catching displays of fresh fruit.

Meats and Seafood:

There are premium meats available, such as hog, chicken, and beef, as well as specialized foods like sausages and cured meats. A wide variety of fresh catches from the Gulf of Mexico and other regions are available at the seafood vendors.

Baked Goods and Specialty Items:
Local honey, handmade jams, and hand-crafted spices are just a few of the unique goods offered by other vendors, while artisan bakers supply a variety of bread, pastries, and sweets. A veritable gold mine of regional goods, the market also includes vendors offering flowers, handcrafted handicrafts, and other specialty things.

Community Events:
The Soulard Farmers Market serves as more than simply a place to shop; it also serves as a gathering place for the community by hosting a range of events. Every visit is a different experience thanks to the vibrant environment created by seasonal festivals, live music events, and cuisine demos.

Soulard Mardi Gras

Soulard has one of the biggest Mardi Gras celebrations in the country every year, which is one of its most well-known occasions. Every year, hundreds of thousands of people attend this colorful event, which takes place in the weeks preceding Lent. Live music, Cajun and Creole food, parades, and various activities like the Grand Parade and the Taste of Soulard are all part of the celebrations. The vibrant and vibrant Soulard Mardi Gras festival captures the vivacious energy and French history of the area.

Soulard Oktoberfest

The Soulard Oktoberfest is a well-liked occasion that honors German customs and culture. This fall event offers German cuisine, music, and of course, beer. In addition to engaging in entertaining activities like stein-holding competitions and dancing performances, guests may savor authentic bratwursts, pretzels, and other German specialties while listening to live polka bands.

Eating and Entertainment

Soulard's vibrant food and nightlife scenes are well-known. Numerous eateries, music venues, and pubs that suit a variety of preferences can be found in the neighborhood:

McGurk's Irish Pub:
A popular hangout for both residents and tourists is McGurk's Irish Pub. McGurk's is well-known for its large outside patio and live Irish music. It also has a menu full of substantial pub cuisine and a cozy, friendly ambiance.

Ninth Street Deli:
This deli, which is part of the Soulard Farmers Market, is a well-liked place to get a tasty bite to eat. For foodies, Ninth Street Deli is a must-visit, especially for its sandwiches and regional delicacies.

Molly's in Soulard:
This lively restaurant and bar has a lovely garden where guests can savor Cajun-inspired cuisine and cool beverages. It's a great place for a night out because of the nice staff and energetic environment.

The Cat's Meow:
A popular dive bar that provides a genuine Soulard experience is The Cat's Meow. The Cat's Meow is the ideal neighborhood pub because of its welcoming atmosphere, reasonably priced beverages, and nice customers.

1860 Saloon:
This popular blues and rock venue features live music every evening. The pub is a terrific spot for entertainment and dining since it delivers a wide range of American and Cajun cuisine.

Culture & Arts

With a multitude of galleries, studios, and cultural establishments, Soulard boasts a flourishing arts and culture scene.

The Great Grizzly Bear:
This location presents live music and events and gives regional musicians and artists a platform. The varied schedule of events guarantees that there's always something fresh and fascinating to take in.

Art Galleries:
Soulard is home to several art galleries that display the creations of regional artists in a variety of media and styles. These galleries provide the chance to buy original artwork and discover St. Louis' artistic abilities.

Cultural Institutions:
Soulard's rich history is conserved through a variety of cultural institutions and historical sites that provide insight into the neighborhood's past and its importance to St. Louis.

Community and Events

The various events and activities that Soulard hosts to bring neighbors and guests together demonstrate the town's strong feeling of community:

Soulard Market Park:
This open area next to the Farmers Market is a well-liked destination for gatherings, picnics, and outdoor recreation. The park is a family-friendly location because of its playground and open areas.

Soulard Art Fair:
Every year, the Soulard Art Fair presents the creations of regional artists and craftspeople, providing an extensive array of original artwork, jewelry, and handcrafted products. The fair is a pleasant family event that also includes food vendors, live music, and kid-friendly activities.

Neighborhood Associations:
To preserve the neighborhood's historic beauty and promote a sense of community, Soulard's vibrant neighborhood groups plan a variety

of activities and events. These groups are essential to maintaining the neighborhood's identity and helping out small businesses.

A Guide for Visitors

With the following information, organizing a trip to Soulard and the Farmers Market is simple:

Market Hours:
Open Wednesday through Saturday, with hours that change daily, is the Soulard Farmers Market. With the market open from early morning until mid-afternoon, Saturday is usually the busiest and most energetic day.

Getting There:
You can easily get to Soulard via car, bicycle, or public transit. Parking is plentiful both in and around the neighborhood of the Farmers Market. It's also simple to explore the region on foot because it's pedestrian-friendly.

Accommodations:
While there aren't any hotels in Soulard itself, downtown St. Louis is a short drive away and has a variety of lodging options to fit a variety of tastes and price ranges.

Soulard embodies the essence of the St. Louis experience with its active Farmers Market, historic charm, and thriving neighborhood. Soulard provides an exciting and distinctive experience that represents the rich cultural fabric of St. Louis, whether you're browsing the market's different wares, dining at one of the neighborhood's numerous restaurants, or taking part in one of its well-known events. It's a location where tradition and modernity collide, and the essence of the neighborhood permeates every area. A trip to Soulard and its farmers market is an experience that delves deeply into St. Louis, offering more than simply a sightseeing opportunity.

Lafayette Square

With a history that stretches back to the middle of the 19th century, Lafayette Square is one of St. Louis's most picturesque and oldest districts. Dedicated after the American Revolutionary War hero Marquis de Lafayette, the region is centered around the gorgeous Lafayette Park, which dates back to 1836 and is the oldest public park west of the Mississippi River. The area prospered throughout the Victorian era and developed into a chic enclave for the city's upper class. Lafayette Square is renowned today for both its thriving sense of community and its exquisitely restored Victorian buildings.

Beauties of Architecture

The magnificent collection of Victorian-era mansions in Lafayette Square, which are renowned for their elaborate designs and elaborate decorations, is what makes the area unique. Numerous architectural styles, such as Second Empire, Italianate, and Romanesque Revival, may be seen throughout the area. These houses provide a visually striking cityscape with their towering windows, ornate cornices, and mansard roofs. With a different architectural marvel around every turn, strolling around Lafayette Square is like taking a trip through time.

Main Draws and Highlights

Lafayette Park

Lafayette Park, a 30-acre green area that provides a peaceful respite from the bustle of the city, lies at the center of the neighborhood. With its meandering walkways, verdant gardens, and tranquil ponds, the park is the ideal place for leisurely walks and picnics. Additionally, it organizes a variety of activities all year long, such as festivals, concerts, and get-togethers with the local community.

Monuments and Statues:
There are several noteworthy monuments in the park, such as a bronze bust of Lafayette and a statue of George Washington. These monuments enhance the park's historical significance and appeal, as do the exquisitely designed gardens and the old bandstand.

Recreation and Relaxation:
There are a variety of recreational activities available at Lafayette Park for visitors to partake in, including biking, running, bird viewing, and fishing in the park's pond. The well-kept playground in the park is popular with families since it gives kids an enjoyable and safe atmosphere.

Victorian Homes Tour

The opportunity to tour Lafayette Square's historic residences is one of the attractions. Every year, the area offers a Victorian Homes Tour that allows guests to tour some of the most exquisitely restored and conserved homes. This event highlights the lavish lifestyles of the wealthy elite of St. Louis in the 19th century and highlights the period's magnificent architecture.

Dining and Shopping

A variety of elegant eateries, welcoming cafés, and distinctive shops can be found in Lafayette Square's bustling eating and retail district.

Eleven Eleven Mississippi:
Part of the renowned eating scene, Eleven Eleven Mississippi offers a delectable fusion of Northern Italian and Californian food. Both residents and tourists adore this restaurant because of its cozy, rustic atmosphere and superb wine selection.

Vin de Set:
With a gorgeously renovated building as its home, Vin de Set serves French-inspired cuisine and has breathtaking city views from its rooftop. A casual meal with friends or a romantic evening is ideal on the rooftop bar and dining area.

Polite Society:
This stylish restaurant serves modern American fare prepared with ingredients that are acquired locally. Its menu is varied. It's a fantastic option for any event because of its chic décor and friendly vibe.

Park Avenue Coffee:
With its well-known gooey butter cake, Park Avenue Coffee is a must-go-to-place for all sugar lovers. Along with pastries and small meals, the café serves a selection of coffee drinks.

Lafayette Square Marketplace:
This quaint market offers a variety of regional sellers offering handcrafted crafts, artisanal products, and fresh fruit. You may grab a bite to eat at one of the food vendors or purchase interesting mementos from this location.

Culture & Arts

Lafayette Square boasts a flourishing arts community, showcasing the neighborhood's creative energy through galleries, studios, and cultural events.

SqWires Annex:
Art exhibits, live music, and community events are held in this event area, which is housed in a restored historic structure. A center of activity in the area, the nearby SqWires Restaurant and Market serves up excellent food and locally sourced goods.

Pop-Up Art Galleries:
Lafayette Square holds several pop-up art galleries and open studio events all year long where guests may view and interact with local artists. These activities demonstrate how dedicated the community is to fostering and advancing the arts.

Outdoor Concerts and Festivals:
Lafayette Park serves as the location for several outdoor concerts and festivals that showcase regional artists and musicians. Attending

these events is a wonderful opportunity to take in the vibrant cultural environment of the area and spend a lovely day entertaining yourself.

Community and Events

The many events and activities that Lafayette Square hosts to unite locals and guests demonstrate the area's strong feeling of community:

House and Garden Tour:
Aside from the Victorian Homes Tour, Lafayette Square organizes an annual House and Garden Tour that highlights the neighborhood's exquisitely designed gardens and historically significant residences. Gardening aficionados and fans of architecture may discover some of the neighborhood's best-kept secrets during this event.

Lafayette Square Spring Fling:
This yearly event welcomes the approach of spring with a lineup of live acts, food vendors, and kid-friendly events. It's a wonderful opportunity to take advantage of the lovely weather and the lively neighborhood vibe.

Holiday Parlor Tour:
The Holiday Parlor Tour offers guests a chance to see the neighborhood's historic homes that have been exquisitely adorned for the holidays. It takes place during the holiday season. This is a great opportunity to see Lafayette Square's warmth and charm while getting into the holiday spirit.

A Guide for Visitors

With the following information, visiting Lafayette Square may be easily planned:

Getting There:
It's simple to get to Lafayette Square by car, bicycle, or public transit. The neighborhood has plenty of street parking and is simple to explore on foot because it is a pedestrian-friendly location.

Hotels:
Although there aren't any hotels right near Lafayette Square, downtown St. Louis is a short drive away and has a variety of lodging options to fit a variety of tastes and price ranges.

Optimal Seasons for Visitation:
Lafayette Square is stunning all year round, but the gardens are at their peak in the spring and summer when outdoor activities are in full force. The neighborhood's festive atmosphere is especially delightful around the holidays.

The area of Lafayette Square exhibits a masterful fusion of design, history, and communal spirit. Lafayette Square provides guests with a singular and fascinating experience, from its magnificent Victorian residences and serene park to its lively eating and cultural activities. Lafayette Square welcomes you to experience its ageless beauty and friendly environment, whether you're strolling around the charming streets, dining at a neighborhood restaurant, or taking part in one of the numerous community activities. The community's pride and enthusiasm are apparent wherever you look on this site where history comes to life.

Central West End

In the center of St. Louis, the Central West End (CWE) is another hidden treasure, renowned for its colorful ambiance, rich history, and diverse array of activities. Artists, authors, and inventors have been drawn to this neighborhood's bustling streets since the early 20th century when it was a center of refinement and culture. Originating with the World's Fair in 1904, the Central West End has developed into a vibrant neighborhood that skillfully combines old-world elegance and contemporary energy.

Beauties of Architecture

It's like embarking on a trip through architectural history as you stroll through the Central West End. There are many different architectural types in the area, ranging from sleek modern structures to huge mansions and majestic townhouses. Several of the old mansions include wonderful elements like elaborate ironwork, elaborate façade, and exquisitely designed gardens. The mix of architectural styles produces a setting that is both visually exciting and appealing to history lovers and fans of modern design.

Eating and Entertainment

The Central West End is well known for its thriving nightlife and eating scenes, which provide a wide range of choices to suit every desire and taste:

Brasserie by Niche:
In the center of the Central West End, Brasserie by Niche is a French bistro with a menu full of traditional French fare and a warm, welcoming ambiance. Especially well-liked is the outside dining area, which makes for an ideal place to dine slowly and people-watch.

The Tenderloin Room:
Known for its exquisite design and flawless service, The Tenderloin Room is an elite steakhouse housed within the historic Chase Park Plaza Hotel. For a work meal or a special night out, it's a fantastic option.

Taste Bar:
A local favorite, Taste Bar is a stylish cocktail bar known for its creative concoctions and small bites. It's the ideal place for a night out with friends or on a date because of the cozy atmosphere and creatively made drinks.

Kingside Diner:
This laid-back eatery provides traditional American comfort cuisine in a classic setting for a more laid-back eating experience. Any time of day, it's a terrific spot for brunch, breakfast, or a quick lunch.

Straub's:
This neighborhood supermarket is well-known for its premium goods and gourmet selections. It is situated in the center of the Central West End. It's a terrific spot to pick up specialty foods for a prepared supper or picnic materials.

Shopping and Boutiques

With a vast array of boutiques, galleries, and specialized shops, the Central West End is a shoppers' paradise:

Left Bank Books:
For more than half a century, this independent bookshop has been a mainstay of the Central West End, providing bookworms with a well-chosen array of books, author events, and a warm and inviting environment.

Q Boutique:
Situated inside the World Chess Hall of Fame, Q Boutique provides a distinctive array of gifts, artwork, and accessories with a chess theme. Chess fans and those searching for unusual mementos should check it out.

Ivy Hill Boutique:
This hip store has a variety of chic apparel, accouterments, and home goods. Fashion-forward customers love it because of the well-curated inventory and welcoming personnel.

Duane Reed Gallery:
Showcasing modern artwork from both regional and national artists, the Duane Reed Gallery is sure to delight art enthusiasts. The gallery showcases a wide variety of media, such as mixed media, painting, and sculpture.

Cultural Institutions

Several cultural establishments that contribute to the lively ambiance of the Central West End are located there:

World Chess Hall of Fame:
The World Chess Hall of Fame is a one-of-a-kind museum honoring the games' cultural relevance and historical background. The museum's chess-themed cafe offers visitors the opportunity to play games, discover rare relics, and peruse intriguing exhibitions.

The Muny:
The biggest outdoor musical theater in the US is The Muny, which is located close by in Forest Park. It offers excellent shows in a lovely outdoor setting and stages a variety of acts every summer.

Pulitzer Arts Foundation:
The Pulitzer Arts Foundation is a contemporary art exhibition and program venue that is conveniently located in the Central West End. Renowned architect Tadao Ando created a minimalist structure for the foundation that is in and of itself a work of art.

Events and Festivals

The vibrant festivals and activities held in the Central West End are well-known for uniting the locals and drawing tourists from far and wide.

Central West End Cocktail Party:
This yearly gathering has a ton of drinks, live music, and food vendors to celebrate the neighborhood's lively bar culture. Discover the finest of Central West End in a lively and enjoyable way.

CWE Halloween Party:
One of the biggest and most well-liked Halloween events in St. Louis is the CWE Halloween Party, which is held in October. The events provide a lively and eerie ambiance for people of all ages, with a costume contest, live entertainment, and a parade.

CWE House Tour:
This yearly occasion provides a unique window into some of the most exquisite and historically significant residences in the area. The tour

showcases the Central West End's historical significance and architectural diversity.

A Guide for Visitors

With the following information, organizing a trip to the Central West End is simple:

Getting There:
It's simple to get to the Central West End by car, bicycle, or public transit. The Central West End station on the MetroLink light rail line is a convenient stop that provides excellent service to the neighborhood. There is also a lot of street parking as well as garage parking.

Rooms:
The area provides a variety of lodging options, including opulent hotels like The Chase Park Plaza and quaint bed & breakfasts. Guests staying in the Central West End have the opportunity to fully experience the lively environment of the neighborhood.

Optimal Seasons for Visitatio:
Although the Central West End is active all year round, spring and fall offer especially nice temperatures and a plethora of outdoor activities. The area is especially lively during the holidays, with magnificently adorned streets and unique activities.

A vibrant area, the Central West End skillfully blends old-world beauty with contemporary dynamism. Its breathtaking architecture, wide range of culinary selections, distinctive retail opportunities, and extensive cultural programs make it one of St. Louis's must-see locations. The Central West End welcomes you to experience its distinct fusion of refinement and excitement, whether you're strolling along its historic streets, dining at a neighborhood restaurant, or taking in one of the numerous events held there. Here, the past and present mix together to create a vibrant community that is friendly to both locals and visitors.

Chapter 6

Forest Park: Trails and Recreational Activities

Being a vital component of St. Louis's identity, Forest Park is more than just a green area. With 1,326 acres, it is larger than Central Park in New York and has been a popular tourist attraction since it opened in 1876. The rich history of Forest Park is matched by the wide range of activities it provides. Forest Park hosted the World's Fair in 1904. Forest Park offers a variety of outdoor activities that are appropriate for people of all ages and interests, from leisurely walks and breathtaking bike rides to golfing and boating.

Trails and Walking Paths

Forest Park Trail System

Walking, running, and cycling enthusiasts will find a vast network of trails throughout the park. The trails meander through many environments, ranging from open fields and forests to historic sites and aquatic features.

Dual Path:
A 5.6-mile loop known as the Dual Path Circles features distinct lanes for bikers and walkers, guaranteeing a fun and safe experience for all users. Wheelchairs and strollers can go along the well-maintained, paved route.

Steinberg Skating Rink Loop:
This is a shorter loop that is very busy during the winter when the rink is open. There are lovely views of the park's natural splendor from the surrounding region.

Jefferson Lake Loop:
A favorite for those seeking a quiet, introspective stroll, this 1.2-mile loop provides lovely views of Jefferson Lake. The lake draws a wide range of bird species, making it an excellent place to go bird-watching.

Trails for Hiking

Forest Park has several hiking routes that go through more natural areas for people looking for a rougher outdoor experience:

Fiddlehead Fern trail:
Offering a more private and personal nature experience, this short, half-mile track winds through a deep forest. This is an excellent trail for families and people seeking a quick yet engaging trip.

Post-Dispatch Lake Trail:
This 1.5-mile walk around Post-Dispatch Lake provides breathtaking views of the surrounding water. It is a little bit longer. Even on hot days, hiking on the route is enjoyable because of the large trees that provide shade.

Recreational Activities

Boating and Fishing

Many lakes and other water features may be found in Forest Park, providing fantastic boating and fishing possibilities.

Boathouse in Forest Park:
On Post-Dispatch Lake, the Boathouse rents out kayaks, canoes, and paddle boats. Visitors may witness wildlife and beautiful views that aren't visible from the beach when boating on the lake, which offers a unique viewpoint of the park. There's also a restaurant at The Boathouse with a great lakefront eating area.

Jefferson Lake:
Well-known for its fantastic fishing, Jefferson Lake is home to several fish species, such as bass, catfish, and sunfish. For those under 16, there is no need for a fishing license, and the lake is always available for fishing.

Golfing

Forest Park is home to the well-regarded Norman K. Probstein Golf Course, a public golf course.

Course Layout:
The golf course consists of three distinct nine-hole courses that may be played in different configurations, offering players of all ability levels a flexible and demanding experience. Rolling fairways, well-placed bunkers, and picturesque water hazards abound on this immaculately kept course.

Driving Range and Lessons:
The facility offers private lessons with qualified teachers in addition to the main course and a driving range. This makes it an excellent spot for novice players to pick up the basics of the game or for seasoned players to hone their techniques.

Tennis and Racquet Sports

Additionally, there are top-notch tennis facilities in Forest Park:

Dwight Davis Tennis Center:
This facility, which has 19 lighted courts with both clay and hard surfaces, is named for the St. Louis native who founded the Davis Cup. All year long, the facility offers instruction and clinics to players of all ages and skill levels, in addition to hosting several competitions and events.

Racquetball and Handball Courts:
The park has several public racquetball and handball courts for anyone interested in playing. These well-kept courts offer a stimulating and enjoyable exercise.

Picnicking and Barbecues

With many dedicated picnic sites and BBQ spots, Forest Park is a great place for outdoor events and picnics.

Picnic Shelters:

Several reservation-only picnic shelters with tables and grills are available throughout the park. Birthday celebrations, get-togethers with friends, and family reunions are perfect occasions to host these shelters.

Open Meadows:
There's plenty of space to spread out a blanket and have a meal in the park's open meadows, perfect for an unplanned picnic outdoors. There are playgrounds and other facilities nearby, and many of these spots have beautiful vistas.

Playgrounds and Splash Pads

There are many things to keep young children occupied for families with children:

Dennis & Judith Jones Visitor and Education Center Playground:
The expansive, contemporary Dennis & Judith Jones Visitor and Education Center Playground has equipment appropriate for kids of all ages. Restrooms and a food and drink shop are available at the neighboring tourist center.

Muny Kids Play Garden:
Conveniently situated close to the Muny outdoor theater, this imaginative play place offers lots of room for kids to run about and have fun, along with interactive sculptures and water elements.

Splash Pads:
A wonderful method for youngsters to cool down during the summer is in one of the park's various splash pads. Younger guests may spend hours of amusement in these well-kept and safe water play facilities.

Seasonal Activities

Winter Sports

Forest Park becomes a winter paradise when the weather becomes cold, with attractions like:

Steinberg Skating Rink:
This outdoor ice skating rink is a well-liked wintertime attraction that provides lessons, skate rentals, and public skating sessions. Open from November through February, the rink has a quaint café where guests may unwind with hot chocolate and nibbles.

Cross-Country Skiing:
The park's wide areas and paths are ideal for cross-country skiing following a snowfall. Bring your gear, and go at your leisure through the park's icy settings.

Events During the Summer

Forest Park hosts a range of events and activities during the summer months, including:

Shakespeare in the Park:
The Saint Louis Shakespeare Festival hosts free outdoor plays in the park every summer. Thousands of people attend this cherished event each year to take in top-notch theater in a stunning environment.

Forest Park Balloon Race:
Held annually in September, this is one of the park's most famous events. There are activities for all ages, live entertainment, food vendors, and dozens of hot air balloons during the festival. Seeing the balloons take off over the park is the event's most spectacular sight.

Festivals and Concerts:
Throughout the summer, Forest Park holds a ton of family-friendly festivals, concerts, and community activities. In the park, events ranging from fitness classes and outdoor movie evenings to music and cuisine festivals are often held.

Visitor Details

With the following information, visiting Forest Park may be easily planned:

Getting There:
You can easily get to Forest Park via vehicle, bicycle, or public transit. With two handy stops at the park's eastern and western boundaries, the MetroLink light rail system provides excellent service to the park. There is plenty of parking accessible within and near the park.

Park Hours:
Forest Park is open every day from dawn to dusk. It's a good idea to verify in advance as certain park attractions and services may have varying hours of operation.

Accessibility:
Paved walkways, handicapped parking spots, and accessible facilities make the park accessible to people of all abilities. Accessible amenities and attractions abound at the park, catering to the needs of those with disabilities.

Visitor Centers:
The Dennis & Judith Jones Visitor and Education Center, which provides exhibits, maps, and information on the park's history and attractions, is a terrific place to start your tour.

St. Louis's Forest Park is a landmark that provides a variety of outdoor experiences for tourists of all ages and interests. Forest Park offers an abundance of options for leisure and relaxation, whether you're strolling along the picturesque pathways, taking a leisurely boat trip, playing golf, or just lounging with a picnic. A must-visit location for anybody wishing to take advantage of the finest that St. Louis has to offer outdoors, it has a rich history, breathtaking scenery, and a wide range of activities.

Missouri Botanical Garden

In the center of St. Louis, the Missouri Botanical Garden, often known as Shaw's Garden, is a veritable sanctuary. It is a National Historic Landmark and one of the oldest botanical gardens in the United States, having been founded in 1859 by philanthropist Henry Shaw. The 79-acre park is well-known for its magnificent floral displays, vast plant collections, and dedication to botanical conservation and study. It gives guests a tranquil getaway from the bustle of the city and an opportunity to commune with nature while taking in the splendor and diversity of the plant world.

The Garden's Layout and Key Attractions

Climatron

The Climatron, a tropical rainforest habitat housed in a geodesic dome conservatory, is one of the most recognizable buildings in the Missouri Botanical Garden. Explore meandering paths surrounded by towering trees, vivid flowers, and lush foliage within the Climatron. With streams, waterfalls, and exotic plants from all over the world, the climate-controlled setting simulates a lowland rainforest. It's a very immersive experience that carries guests away to a tropical haven.

Japanese Garden

One of the biggest Japanese walking gardens in North America is the Japanese Garden, sometimes called Seiwa-en. This 14-acre park, created by landscape architect Koichi Kawana, has classic characteristics including calm ponds, arching bridges, well-pruned trees, and beautifully raked gravel. The garden allows guests to slow down and take in the harmony and balance of Japanese garden design. It is a haven of peace and reflection. Cherry blooms in the spring and vivid maple leaves in the fall are examples of seasonal highlights.

Victorian District

A delightful section of the garden that highlights Victorian-era gardening techniques and ideas is called the Victorian District. Highlights include the Victorian Garden, with its elaborate fountains, period-perfect garden structures, and heritage flowers, as well as Henry Shaw's restored country mansion, Tower Grove House. This section emphasizes the historical significance of the garden and offers a fascinating look into the past.

Children's Garden

Families with little children should make time to visit the Doris I. Schnuck Children's Garden. With practical exercises and play spaces, this interactive garden aims to captivate and inform children about the natural world. A treehouse, a splash area, a cave, and themed gardens that delve into various ecosystems and habitats are among the features. The Children's Garden is an enjoyable and instructive experience for the whole family since it promotes inquiry and discovery.

Rose Garden

A magnificent display of over 3,000 roses, spanning over 300 types, may be found at the Gladney Rose Garden. With its vivid hues and enticing scents, this formal garden is a sensory feast. Many rose varieties, such as hybrid teas, floribundas, grandifloras, and climbers, may be found in the well-kept Rose Garden. It's the ideal location for a romantic moment or a stroll.

Temperate House

Many different kinds of plants from all over the world's temperate zones may be found in the Temperate House. Numerous species may be found in this glasshouse, ranging from South African bulbs and Chilean perennials to Mediterranean shrubs and Australian wildflowers. A unique botanical experience is offered by the regulated atmosphere, which enables the production of plants that do well in milder climes.

Highlights and Events

Spring Blooms

At the Missouri Botanical Garden, springtime is a magnificent season when the scenery bursts into a riot of color. Beautiful displays of tulips, daffodils, and hyacinths, along with flowering trees and shrubs, are available for visitors to enjoy. Hundreds of orchids in a dizzying diversity of forms and hues are on display during the annual Orchid Show, which takes place in the Climatron.

Summer Splendor

Vibrant flowers and an abundance of foliage characterize the garden throughout the summer. Live music performances take place in the lovely outdoor setting of the garden on Wednesday nights from May through July during the annual Whitaker Music Festival. Bring a picnic, and take in the scenery and music while doing so.

Fall Foliage

Fall foliage, which transforms trees and bushes into vivid hues of red, orange, and yellow, is a sight to behold. This is the most beautiful time of year to visit the Japanese Garden because the maple trees create a striking contrast to the calm ponds and well-kept grounds. Each year in October, the Best of Missouri Market event features live entertainment, food vendors, and local artists.

Winter Wonders

The Missouri Botanical Garden is inspiring and beautiful even in the cold. With thousands of dazzling lights and festive displays, the garden is transformed into a winter paradise during the yearly Garden Glow event. Visitors may enjoy tropical and temperate plants all year round thanks to the Climatron and Temperate House, which offer a pleasant haven from the cold.

Education and Research

The Missouri Botanical Garden serves as a hub for botanical research and teaching in addition to being a visually stunning location. The study and preservation of plant biodiversity, both locally and worldwide, is one of the garden's goals. A great resource for scholars and students, the Peter H. Raven Library is named for the garden's longstanding director and has a sizable collection of botanical literature.

Workshops, talks, and guided tours are among the educational offerings in the garden that are appropriate for a variety of age groups and areas of interest. To promote a love of the outdoors and an awareness of the value of plant protection, the garden also conducts outreach initiatives and collaborations with educational institutions.

Guided Tours and Costs

By taking one of the many offered guided tours, your experience exploring the Missouri Botanical Garden will be substantially enhanced. Comprehensive information on the history, plant collections, and horticultural techniques of the garden is provided by these visits.

General Garden Tour:
Guided by experienced docents, this tour covers the garden's principal features and gives a summary of its history and primary draws. Tours usually run 60-90 minutes and cost around $12 per person, on top of the standard garden entry price.

Specialty Tours:
These themed tours concentrate on certain sections of the park, such as the Climatron, the Japanese park, or the Victorian District. Specialty trips typically cost $15 per person, which also includes garden entry.

Private Group Tours:

These can be scheduled for a more individualized experience. For parties of ten or more, these excursions usually cost $18 per person, plus entrance, and may be customized to the interests of the group.

Educational Workshops:
The garden hosts a range of seminars and workshops covering subjects including plant identification, botanical art, and gardening practices. Workshop costs vary, but the majority are between $25 and $50 each session.

Information for Visitors

With the following information, visiting the Missouri Botanical Garden may be easily planned:

Location:
Just a short drive from St. Louis's downtown lies the garden, which may be found at 4344 Shaw Boulevard, St. Louis, MO 63110.

Hours:
The Garden Glow seasonal lights show and special events extend the garden's daily hours of operation from 9 a.m. to 5 p.m.

Admission:
Adults pay $14 for general admission, St. Louis City and County residents pay $6, and children under 12 enter free of charge. Additionally, memberships with unlimited annual entrance and other perks are offered.

Accessibility:
The garden is dedicated to giving every guest an accessible experience. Wheelchairs and scooters may be rented, and the majority of the routes are handicapped accessible. There are also accessible parking spaces and facilities.

Eating and Shopping:
In a relaxed atmosphere, Sassafras Café serves a selection of seasonal foods, snacks, and drinks. A large selection of gardening equipment,

books on botany, presents, and mementos are available at The Garden Gate Shop.

A veritable gold mine of botanical beauty, the Missouri Botanical Garden serves as a reminder of the significance of plant conservation and education. For anybody interested in nature and horticulture, it is a must-visit location because of its varied gardens, extensive history, and exciting activities. The Missouri Botanical Garden provides an enlightening and remarkable experience, whether you're strolling down the verdant pathways of the Climatron, seeking tranquility in the Japanese Garden, or learning about the most recent advancements in botanical science.

Riverboat Cruises on the Mississippi

An enduring emblem of American history and culture is the majestic Mississippi River. It has been essential to trade, transportation, and exploration as it flows over 2,300 miles from Minnesota to the Gulf of Mexico. Few other towns have the opportunity to experience the Mississippi as St. Louis does, and that is via riverboat. St. Louis is well situated along this magnificent river. With riverboat excursions, visitors may take in the picturesque scenery, discover the history of the river, and get a fresh perspective on the city's skyline. Riverboat cruises provide a nostalgic trip through time.

Types of Riverboat Cruises

Sightseeing Cruises

For those who like to enjoy the sounds and sights of the Mississippi River while learning about the background and significance of St. Louis, sightseeing cruises are ideal. These trips range between sixty and ninety minutes, and the skilled guides recount interesting anecdotes about the city, the river, and important monuments.

Gateway Arch Riverboats:
Offering breathtaking views of the Arch, the St. Louis skyline, and the historic Eads Bridge, these excursions depart from the riverside close to the Gateway Arch. Adult tickets typically cost $24 while children's tickets cost $14. Seniors and organizations can receive discounts on their tickets.

Dinner Cruises

Dinner cruises provide an idyllic, romantic, and carefree evening on the lake, replete with delectable cuisine, live music, and dancing. A full-course dinner with variations to accommodate different tastes and dietary concerns is served during these two to three-hour excursions.

Gateway Arch Riverboats Dinner Cruise:
The Gateway Arch Riverboats Dinner Cruise is a well-liked choice that offers a buffet cooked by a chef, live music, and stunning sunset views across the Mississippi River. Depending on the menu and season, the price ranges from $50 to $70 per person.

Themed Cruises

With the addition of special events, activities, and entertainment, themed cruises provide a distinctive take on the typical riverboat experience. These excursions offer a lively and entertaining way to see the river, complete with historical reenactments and seasonal festivities.

Blues Cruise:
The Blues Cruise honors St. Louis's rich musical past and showcases live blues performances by regional artists. While sailing down the river, visitors may take in the melancholic blues sounds. The usual cost of a ticket is $25 to $35 per person.

Haunted Halloween Cruise:
This terrifying Halloween cruise is ideal for thrill-seekers and families. It has ghost stories, eerie décor, and entertaining

kid-friendly activities. Typically, adult tickets cost $20, while kid tickets cost $15.

The Best Parts of a Riverboat Cruise

Historic Eads Bridge

Seeing the Eads Bridge up close is one of the attractions of every riverboat ride. The Eads Bridge, which was the first steel bridge built across the Mississippi River and was finished in 1874, is still a wonder of engineering. Exciting information on the bridge's construction and importance in American history is frequently shared by the guides as the boat goes beneath it.

Gateway Arch

Without breathtaking views of the Gateway Arch, a riverboat trip in St. Louis would not be complete. At 630 feet, the Arch stands as the highest man-made monument in the United States and represents the nation's westward development. There are amazing photo opportunities and a distinct viewpoint while viewing the Arch from the river.

The Ecology of the Mississippi River

Learning about the Mississippi River's environment is another benefit of taking a riverboat tour. While pointing out local animals like bald eagles, egrets, and herons, guides frequently talk about the river's varied ecosystem. By assisting passengers in appreciating the river's natural beauty and environmental significance, this educational component enriches the experience.

St. Louis Skyline

Passengers get expansive views of the St. Louis cityscape as the boat glides along the river. From the sea, one can view iconic structures like the Old Courthouse, the Wainwright Building, and the Cathedral

Basilica, which contrast sharply with the city's contemporary construction.

Planning Your Cruise

Make a Reservation and Book It:
Reservations should be made well in advance for your riverboat trip to guarantee a seamless and pleasurable experience, particularly during the busiest travel seasons and for specialty-themed cruises. Either at the ticket office next to the Arch or online at the Gateway Arch Riverboats website, tickets may be bought.

Items to Pack:
To make the most of your riverboat journey, think about packing the following things:

- Camera: To record the breathtaking vistas and priceless experiences.

- Sunscreen and Hat: Wear a hat and sunscreen on daytime voyages to avoid sunburn.

- Comfy Clothing and Shoes: Since the boat decks might be windy, it's a good idea to wear comfy shoes and layers of clothing.

- Binoculars: To observe birds and get a closer look at far-off landmarks.

Accessibility

With ramps and special seating sections for visitors with mobility issues, the majority of riverboat trips are wheelchair accessible. It's advised to get in touch with the cruise line operator ahead of time if you need specific accommodations to guarantee a seamless trip.

A memorable and distinctive way to see St. Louis is through riverboat rides on the Mississippi. There is a cruise choice to fit any preference, whether it be for history, music, or just taking in the river's picturesque splendor. An unforgettable experience is created when breathtaking scenery, captivating storytelling, and the nostalgic allure of riverboats come together. You'll understand the Mississippi River's significance in building the city and the country better as you cruise down its waters, adding to the richness and significance of your trip to St. Louis.

Chapter 7

Catching a Cardinals Game at Busch Stadium

More than simply a baseball field, Busch Stadium—home of the St. Louis Cardinals—is a vital part of the city's character and a must-see location for sports fans. The third stadium to carry the Busch brand opened its doors in 2006. Located in the center of downtown St. Louis, it offers breathtaking views of the Gateway Arch and the surrounding skyline. Fans of the Cardinals and other sports enthusiasts love the stadium because of its unique architecture, which blends contemporary conveniences with a vintage baseball atmosphere.

The Cardinals' Background and Significance

With a long history that stretches back to 1882, the St. Louis Cardinals are among Major League Baseball's most illustrious teams. The Cardinals are second only to the New York Yankees in World Series victories gained over the years, with many pennants in the National League. Legendary athletes like Stan Musial, Bob Gibson, and Ozzie Smith, whose contributions to the game have irrevocably changed the sport, are part of the team's heritage. Going to a Cardinals game at Busch Stadium is an experience that involves more than just baseball; it's about seeing a custom that has been preserved by fans for centuries.

Game Day Experience

Atmosphere and Fan Culture

Busch Stadium has an electrifying ambiance that is lively and inviting due to the sea of red-clad supporters. The finest baseball fans are those who follow the Cardinals because of their devoted following and extensive knowledge of the team. An amazing atmosphere is created by the fan base's friendship, the intensity of the match, and their mutual passion for the team.

Seating Options and the Stadium Layout

Busch Stadium can accommodate more than 45,000 people and has a range of seating options to accommodate a range of tastes and price points. Everybody may find their ideal experience, be it the closeness of the field-level seats, the expansive vistas from the upper decks, or the opulence of a suite. With its food, entertainment, and retail options, the Ballpark Village, which is next to the stadium, improves game day festivities.

Food and Beverage Offerings

Delicious and varied food options are one of the best parts about going to a game at Busch Stadium. There is much to choose from, including St. Louis-style pizza and toasted ravioli, as well as regional staples like popcorn, nachos, and hot dogs. To ensure that visitors may have a full dining experience, the stadium also serves a selection of craft beers and specialty beverages.

Entertainment and Activities

To keep people interested after the game, Busch Stadium provides a variety of entertainment alternatives. A playground, batting cage, and interactive activities make the Family Pavilion in Ford Plaza an excellent place for families with kids. Fans may unwind and enjoy the game in a vibrant atmosphere on the Budweiser Terrace, which has communal seating spaces and live music.

Special Events and Promotions

Giveaway Nights

Giveaway evenings are a regular event for the Cardinals when fans can pick up exclusive merchandise including caps, jerseys, and bobbleheads. The thrill of game day is increased by these well-liked festivities. To find out what freebies are available when you arrive, make sure to check the promotional calendar beforehand.

Theme Nights

The Cardinals' program highlights include theme nights, which provide distinctive experiences based on certain groups or topics. Events honoring first responders and members of the armed forces, as well as Star Wars and Margaritaville Nights, are just a few examples of the themed prizes and special entertainment that take place on these nights.

Fireworks After the Game

The St. Louis skyline is illuminated by the Cardinals' post-game fireworks displays on certain Saturdays. An evening at the ballgame is perfectly capped off by these amazing performances, which are set to music. Plan appropriately if you want to see a fireworks show; they are particularly well-liked during the summer and on holidays.

Guided Tours and Behind-the-Scenes Experiences

On days when there are no games, guided tours are offered for individuals who desire a more in-depth look at the background and internal operations of Busch Stadium. These tours provide guests access to locations that are normally off-limits to the public, such as the press box, the dugout, and the Cardinals clubhouse. They also take tourists behind the scenes.

Cardinals Hall of Fame and Museum:
The Cardinals Hall of Fame and Museum is a must-see for every baseball enthusiast. It is situated in Ballpark Village. Player outfits, World Series trophies, and historical photos are among the many

items kept at the museum. Through interactive exhibitions, fans can relive some of the most iconic events in Cardinals history.

Tour Fees and Schedule:
Prices for guided tours typically range from $20 for adults to $15 for children, with elderly citizens and groups receiving a discounted rate. Making reservations for your trip in advance is a smart idea, particularly during the popular summer months.

Advice for Observing a Game

Purchasing Tickets:
The official MLB website, the Busch Stadium box office, or independent vendors are the three places to get tickets for Cardinals games. It is advisable to compare prices and make advance plans since they might differ based on the opponent, day of the week, and seating arrangement. Weekday matches and games in the early part of the season are usually less expensive and packed.

Moving to the Stadium:
Numerous downtown hotels have easy access to Busch Stadium via automobile, public transportation, and even foot. Fans may easily access the stadium using the MetroLink light rail system, which has a stop there. There are lots and garages surrounding the stadium where parking is accessible, but it's best to arrive early because spaces tend to fill up quickly on game days.

Staying Comfortable :
Take into account the following advice to make sure you have a relaxing and joyful experience:

- Dress Appropriately: The weather in St. Louis is not always predictable, so be sure to check the forecast and wear layers if necessary. Remember to wear your Cardinals apparel to show your team spirit.

- Remain Hydrated: Take use of the stadium's covered sections and cooling facilities, drink lots of water, and remember to stay hydrated because summer games may get hot.

- Arrive Early: Arriving early at the stadium gives you the chance to take in the pre-game excitement, explore Ballpark Village, and visit the team store.

Experiences gained from seeing a St. Louis Cardinals game at Busch Stadium are unique and go beyond baseball. It all comes down to joining a community, honoring a great culture, and making enduring experiences. Whether you're a devoted Cardinals supporter or you're just in town for a visit, you must see a game at Busch Stadium. A Cardinals game promises to be an unforgettable experience that captures the essence of St. Louis's sports culture, from the thunderous cheers of the fans to the sound of the bat.

The Fabulous Fox Theatre

The Fabulous Fox Theatre is an architectural wonder, a cultural center, and one of St. Louis's most beloved icons. It has been captivating audiences for almost a century. The theater, which is a monument to the city's rich history and continued passion for the performing arts, is situated in the center of the Grand Center Arts District. When it was opened in 1929, the Fox Theatre served as the Fox Film Corporation's movie palace. However, it has since changed to become one of the top locations for live events, including Broadway plays, musicals, dance productions, and more.

Architectural Style

The Fabulous Fox Theatre, created by C. Howard Crane and William Fox, is a magnificent example of Siamese Byzantine architecture. The rich decorations of its luxurious interior include tall columns, elaborate gold-leaf motifs, and a large chandelier that hangs over the whole theater. Every visit to the theater is an unforgettable experience because of its exquisite design, which takes guests to a more opulent and elegant time in history.

Preservation and Repair

To maintain its historic beauty and provide contemporary comforts, the Fox Theatre has undergone many restorations throughout the years. To preserve its beauty and magnificence for future generations, the theater underwent a significant restoration effort in the 1980s that returned it to its previous state of grandeur. Due to its cultural and historical value, the Fox Theatre is now included on the National Register of Historic Places.

Live Performances & Broadway Shows

Some of the largest and most popular Broadway productions have been known to play at the Fabulous Fox Theatre. The Fox offers St. Louis the enchantment of Broadway, showcasing everything from classic Broadway shows like "Les Misérables" and "The Phantom of the Opera" to modern favorites like "Hamilton" and "Wicked." The theater's varied schedule features stand-up comedy shows, dance performances, concerts by top artists, and special events in addition to musicals.

Acoustics and Seating

To allow spectators to fully immerse themselves in the performances, the Fox Theatre's auditorium is intended to offer outstanding sightlines and acoustics from every seat. With more than 4,500 seats, the theater provides a variety of seating arrangements, including orchestra seats near the stage and balcony seats with a broad view of the action.

Amenities and Services

The Fabulous Fox Theatre provides several facilities and services to make the theatergoing experience even more enjoyable. The theater's classy lounges and bars give a relaxing area to unwind before the performance or during intermission, while concession kiosks offer a variety of snacks and drinks. To provide an inclusive and joyful experience for everyone, the theater is also outfitted with accessible seating and amenities for patrons with disabilities.

Educational Programs

Supporting community involvement and arts education is a priority for The Fox Theatre. The theater offers outreach initiatives, workshops, and scholarships to support and develop young performers through organizations like the Fox Performing Arts Charitable Foundation. With the help of these initiatives, everyone should be able to enjoy the arts and develop a lifetime love of music and theater.

Behind the Scenes Tours

The Fabulous Fox Theatre provides guided tours that take guests behind the scenes for those who want to learn more about the history and design of the theater. Viewing the stage, orchestra pit and dressing rooms behind the scenes at the theater is a special privilege offered by these excursions. The history of the theater, its well-known actors, and the intricate details of its construction are all fascinatingly told by tour guides.

- Tours & Schedule: Guided tours typically run between $10 and $20 per person and are available on a few different days. Booking your excursion in advance is advised, particularly during the busiest travel times.

Advice on Seeing a Show

Purchasing Tickets:
You may buy tickets for shows at the Fabulous Fox Theatre at the box office, via the official theater website, or from accredited ticket resellers. To guarantee the best seats and rates, get your tickets in advance. Prices vary based on the show, seating arrangement, and date.

Moving to the Theater:
Because of its prime location in the Grand Center Arts District, the Fabulous Fox Theatre is easily accessible from surrounding hotels and restaurants by car, public transportation, and foot. Parking is accessible in several lots and garages surrounding the theater, but it's advisable to arrive early because, on show nights, spots might fill up rapidly.

Proper Clothes and Manners:
Although there isn't a set dress requirement to attend shows at the Fox Theatre, many patrons prefer to look put together, especially for nighttime shows. Although wearing business casual is popular, it's vital to be at ease and considerate to other theatergoers. Turn off your cell phones, arrive on time, and show people consideration while the performance is going on.

More than just a place to enjoy entertainment, the Fabulous Fox Theatre serves as a landmark for the performing arts and a representation of St. Louis' rich cultural legacy. A trip to the Fox Theatre guarantees an amazing experience full of beauty, history, and creative brilliance, whether you're there for a concert, a Broadway production, or a special occasion. You'll be taken to a world of wonder and excitement where the magic of live performance comes to life in the center of St. Louis as soon as you walk through its enormous doors and take a seat in the luxurious auditorium.

Chapter 8

Must-Try Local Foods

The cuisine of St. Louis is a delectable fusion of innovative techniques, local ingredients, and pride. The cuisine of the city is varied and reflects its rich cultural background, ranging from inventive delicacies like toasted ravioli and gooey butter cake to famous sandwiches and BBQ. In this section, we will explore some of the local delicacies that are a must-try and help to define St. Louis's culinary scene.

Toasted Ravioli

Renowned for its flavor, toasted ravioli, or "T-raves," originated in the Italian-American communities of St. Louis and has become a popular local dish. An old Italian neighborhood eatery on The Hill is said to have accidentally developed this crispy pleasure back in the 1940s. The crispy, golden-brown delight that emerged from a chef's accidental drop of ravioli into boiling oil rather than boiling water rapidly became a local favorite.

What Makes It Special:
Toasted ravioli are square or round pasta pockets that have been perfectly deep-fried after being breaded and stuffed with a flavorful meat or cheese combination. The outcome is a soft, delicious inside with a crispy, crunchy shell that contrasts well. The mouthwatering blend of flavors and textures found in toasted ravioli, which is typically served with a side of marinara sauce for dipping, makes it an excellent choice for an appetizer or snack.

Where to Try It:

Though St. Louis has many excellent restaurants, the following are some favorites:

- Charlie Gitto:
  The Hill-based Charlie Gitto is frequently cited as the birthplace of toasted ravioli. With a flavor of the original recipe, the restaurant's rendition is well worth trying.

- Anthonino's Taverna:
  Also located on The Hill, Anthonino's is well-known for its Greek and Italian fare. Served with homemade marinara sauce, their toasted ravioli is a well-liked option, crafted from premium ingredients.

- Imo's Pizza:
  Well-known for its St. Louis-style pizza, Imo's also has delicious toasted ravioli that goes well with their specialty pies.

Gooey Butter Cake

The 1930s saw the invention of gooey butter cake, another famous St. Louis dish. Narratives suggest that the dish originated from an error made by a baker, who inadvertently mixed flour and butter in the wrong amounts, resulting in a cake that was very moist, thick, and sweet. Since then, bakeries and homes in St. Louis have continued to serve this joyful accident, which swiftly gained popularity as a favorite local dessert.

What Makes It Special:
A coating of soft, gooey frosting that melts on your tongue adorns the rich, buttery crust of gooey butter cake. Typically, cream cheese, butter, sugar, and eggs are combined to make the top layer, which has a rich and creamy texture. It is commonly topped with powdered sugar and goes well with chocolate, pumpkin, or fruit as flavorings, but it also tastes well alone.

Where to Try It:

Famous in St. Louis for their luscious butter cake are several bakeries and cafés, such as:

- Gooey Louie:
  This business specializes in gooey butter cake and serves a range of flavors, such as classic, chocolate chip, and seasonal. A delightful experience is guaranteed with every mouthful since each cake is meticulously crafted.

- Park Avenue Coffee:
  Park Avenue Coffee is a chain of coffee shops in St. Louis that specializes in a wide variety of flavors of luscious butter cake. A taste for every palette may be found, ranging from traditional to inventive pairings like red velvet and key lime.

- Russell's on Macklind:
  This little bakery and cafe has received great praise for its delicious take on molten butter cake. Grab a slice to go or enjoy it right now with a cup of coffee.

St. Louis-Style Pizza

With its thin, cracker-like crust, square-cut pieces, and Provel cheese, St. Louis-style pizza stands apart from other regional pizza varieties. This pizza has a distinct creamy smoothness thanks to the melting provel cheese, a special combination of provolone, Swiss, and cheddar. To enhance the taste with each mouthful, the toppings are usually distributed edge-to-edge.

Recommended Location for Trying It:
Pizza in the St. Louis style is best found at Imo's Pizza, often known as "The Square Beyond Compare." Located all around the city, Imo's provides a traditional taste of this local delicacy. Here are some other noteworthy pizzerias:

- Farotto's Italian Restaurant:

The Farotto's Italian Restaurant is a beloved neighborhood eatery in Rock Hill that has been serving delectable pizza in the St. Louis style since 1956.

- Pi Pizzeria:
  Distinguished by its inventive toppings and use of fresh ingredients, Pi Pizzeria puts a distinctive twist on St. Louis-style pizza, whether ordered deep-dish or thin-crust.

St. Paul Sandwich

Chinese-American restaurants in St. Louis are the main source of the St. Paul sandwich, a unique fusion meal. Serve it with pieces of white bread, mayonnaise, lettuce, pickles, and occasionally tomato on top of an egg-foo young patty—a Chinese-style omelet. Because it offers a delectable fusion of flavors and textures, this unusual combination has grown to be a popular local favorite.

What Makes It Special:
A savory egg foo young sandwich paired with the crisp bite of pickles and lettuce, all held together by soft, pillowy bread, makes for a filling and delectable dinner. It is evidence of the city's inventive culinary spirit and its capacity to skillfully combine several ethnic elements to create something distinctly delectable.

Where to Try it:
Excellent St. Paul sandwiches are served in several Chinese-American restaurants in St. Louis, such as:

- Mai Lee:
  Known for its genuine Chinese and Vietnamese food, Mai Lee is located in Brentwood. A notable item on the menu is their St. Paul sandwich.

- Chop Suey Louie's: Choose from a range of St. Paul sandwiches, including chicken, pork, beef, and shrimp varieties, at this traditional Chinese takeout restaurant.

St. Louis Barbecue

The delicious, slow-cooked meats and tart, tomato-based sauce that characterize St. Louis barbecue are well-known. Greater in size and meat content than baby back ribs, the city is especially well-known for its spare ribs. BBQ sauce, which combines sweet and sour notes with smoky aromas, is usually applied after the ribs are barbecued in the St. Louis manner. This results in a delicious dish.

Where to Try it:
Known for its amazing ribs and other smoked meats, some barbecue restaurants in St. Louis include:

- Pappy's Smokehouse:
  A St. Louis mainstay, Pappy's Smokehouse is well-known for its Memphis-style barbecue, which consists of slow-smoked meats with apple and cherry wood cooking. Always a hit with outstanding reviews, their ribs are a must-try.

- Bogart's Smokehouse:
  The Soulard neighborhood's Bogart's Smokehouse is renowned for its creative side dishes and expertly smoked meats. Known for its delectable take on the classic St. Louis barbecue, their apricot-glazed ribs are especially well-liked.

- Sugarfire Smoke House: Located all around the city, Sugarfire Smoke House provides inventive BBQ recipes with a focus on premium, locally sourced ingredients. You should try their pulled pork, brisket, and ribs.

The diversity of foods offered by St. Louis's culinary scene reflects the city's inventive spirit and rich cultural legacy. It is a rich tapestry of flavors and customs. A tribute to the city's culinary inventiveness and pride are its characteristic dishes, which range from the crunchy joy of toasted ravioli to the luscious sweetness of gooey butter cake, as well as the unusual St. Paul sandwich and the perfectly smoky St. Louis-style ribs. A trip to St. Louis wouldn't be complete without sampling these regional delicacies, which give a mouthwatering and unforgettable taste of the city.

Best Places for Craft Beer and Cocktails

German immigration turned St. Louis into a significant beer producer in the 19th century, and the city has had a long and rich brewing heritage since then. The thriving craft beer market and the increasing number of craft cocktail establishments that provide creative and delectable beverages today are testaments to that tradition. Whatever your beverage preference—beer or cocktails—St. Louis offers a wide selection of places to satisfy your thirst.

Top Craft Breweries

Schlafly Tap Room

The oldest craft brewery in St. Louis and a pioneer in the community's beer culture, Schlafly Tap Room opened its doors in 1991. Situated in a downtown historic structure, the Tap Room serves a broad selection of beers ranging from traditional varieties like Kolsch and Pale Ale to experimental and seasonal offerings. The brewery is well-liked by both residents and tourists due to its friendly environment and regular live music events.

Urban Chestnut Brewing Company

The Urban Chestnut Brewing Company (UCBC) is renowned for its distinctive brewing methods, which combine contemporary American craft processes with classic European beer types. UCBC serves a wide selection of beers and has two locations in St. Louis: a spacious bierhall in Midtown and a quaint biergarten in The Grove. The brewery's signature beers, Zwickel Bavarian Lager and Schnickelfritz Bavarian Weissbier, are highly recommended, while its

Reverence and Revolution series highlight their skill and inventiveness.

4 Hands Brewing Company

Prominent for its inventive and delectable beers, 4 Hands Brewing Co. is situated close to St. Louis's downtown. While the brewery's seasonal and limited-edition releases provide something fresh and interesting all year long, its core portfolio consists of favorites like Divided Sky Rye IPA and City Wide American Pale Ale. The expansive taproom of the brewery is a terrific location to unwind and have a pint because it offers a range of games and activities.

Perennial Artisan Ales

The goal of Perennial Artisan Ales is to create handcrafted, limited-edition beers that prioritize originality and quality. Renowned for its barrel-aged beers and ales with Belgian influences, Perennial has established a stellar reputation both domestically and abroad. Every year, they especially look forward to and enjoy their Abraxas, an imperial stout made with ancho chili peppers, cacao nibs, vanilla beans, and cinnamon sticks. The South Carondelet neighborhood's brewery tasting room provides a comfortable environment in which to enjoy their unique brews.

Standout Cocktail Bars

Taste Bar

A sanctuary for fans of handmade cocktails, Taste Bar is situated in the Central West End. The bar's skilled mixologists employ premium spirits, fresh ingredients, house-made syrups and bitters, and other components to produce inventive and exquisitely constructed beverages. There's always something new to taste thanks to the menu's constant changes, which combine traditional drinks with creative concoctions. Cocktail fans should visit Taste Bar because of its chic and cozy atmosphere as well as its staff's expertise and friendliness.

Planter's House

Located in Lafayette Square, Planter's House is a classy cocktail bar with a wide selection of beautifully mixed beverages. The bar, which takes its name from the storied Planter's Hotel, honors the rich heritage of St. Louis while providing a chic and contemporary drinking experience. The menu features a selection of expertly and creatively created seasonal specialties, specialty beverages, and classic cocktails. The pub is a great place to have a drink with friends because of its sophisticated yet laid-back ambiance and lovely outside terrace.

The Gin Room

The Gin Room in the South Grand district is a must-see for gin aficionados. This warm and welcoming bar offers an amazing assortment of gins from all over the world and specializes in gin-based drinks. Whether your preference is for a traditional gin and tonic or something a little more daring, skilled bartenders are masters at creating tasty and creative gin beverages. Gin enthusiasts and newbies alike will find a warm and inviting atmosphere at The Gin Room thanks to its laid-back atmosphere and welcoming personnel.

YellowBelly

Yellowbelly is a lively pub and restaurant in the Central West End that blends tropical cuisine with Midwesterner friendliness. The bar's menu of creative seasonal concoctions, tiki-inspired drinks, and rum-based beverages are all available. Popular selections include the Painkiller and Jungle Bird, two of the establishment's signature drinks, and a changing menu means there's always something fresh to try. Yellowbelly is a remarkable and enjoyable place to spend a night out because of its vibrant atmosphere and whimsical design.

Beer and Cocktail Festivals

St. Louis Brewers Heritage Festival

An annual celebration of the city's thriving craft beer culture and rich brewing heritage is the St. Louis Brewers Heritage Festival. The event, which takes place in Forest Park, offers a variety of beers from nearby brewers, including limited releases and unusual collaborations. In addition to sampling a wide variety of varieties, attendees may take in live music and educational workshops and demonstrations that teach them more about the brewing process. For beer lovers who want to sample the finest of St. Louis's craft beer scene, the festival is a must-go event.

IndiHop

Nestled in between Cherokee Street and The Grove is a unique beer and music event called IndiHop. A variety of beers from nearby breweries are available at the event, with host venues being each participating company. Visitors may go between venues while tasting various beers and taking in live musical acts. Discovering St. Louis's dynamic neighborhoods and craft beer sector is made enjoyable and engaging with IndiHop.

St. Louis Cocktail Party

The greatest mixologists and cocktail establishments in the city get together for Cocktail Party St. Louis, an annual event. The event, which takes place in the Central West End, offers a huge selection of specialty drinks, as well as live entertainment, cuisine from neighborhood restaurants, and entertainment. In addition to learning about the craft of mixology, attendees may try specialty cocktails from some of St. Louis's best bartenders and take in the vibrant and festive atmosphere. Discovering the ingenuity and skill of the city's cocktail scene is highly recommended through the Cocktail Party.

For those who want to enjoy a drink, St. Louis's craft beer and cocktail industry provides a vibrant and varied selection. The city offers a wide variety of tastes and experiences, from cutting-edge cocktail bars like Taste and Planter's House to iconic brewers like Schlafly and Urban Chestnut. St. Louis offers a wide variety of beverages that are sure to please and inspire, whether you're enjoying a well-made cocktail or a wonderfully produced beer. A visit to the Gateway City wouldn't be complete without checking out these hidden jewels, which provide a flavor of the dynamic and always-changing culinary scene in the area.

Nightlife Hotspots and Bars

With a variety of nightlife options to suit a wide range of interests and inclinations, St. Louis comes alive after dark. The city has lots to offer, whether your mood calls for a live music performance in a cozy setting, a fun-filled night of dancing at a fashionable club, or a relaxed evening at your local pub. This is a list of some of the best pubs and nightclubs in St. Louis that you should check out.

Washington Avenue

One of the most active areas of the city's nightlife is Washington Avenue, which is found in downtown St. Louis. This busy street is a well-liked hangout for both locals and tourists since it is dotted with bars, clubs, and restaurants.

The Thaxton Speakeasy

The Thaxton Speakeasy, tucked away in a landmark Art Deco structure, transports visitors to the Prohibition era with its retro furnishings and enigmatic ambiance. The exclusivity of this place is increased by the requirement to access it with a password, which is posted on their social media. A wonderful night out is guaranteed with the skillfully made drinks and vibrant atmosphere found within.

The Wheelhouse

The vibrant atmosphere and large area of The Wheelhouse, a bar and nightclub, attract a lot of people. The Wheelhouse has lots of space for socializing and enjoying the evening with its several bars, dance floors, and outside terrace. There's always something going on at this facility because of its many themed parties, live DJ sets, and other events.

The Grove

A lively and varied neighborhood, The Grove is well-known for its varied nightlife. The Grove provides a warm and accepting atmosphere for everyone, including LGBTQ-friendly pubs and artisan cocktail lounges.

The Atomic Cowboy

Atomic Cowboy is a multipurpose space that houses a nightclub, bar, and restaurant under one roof. Atomic Cowboy is a terrific location to start your night with a tasty dinner and a specialty cocktail. It's known for its laid-back vibe and large drink selection. With live music and DJ performances, the area becomes a vibrant dance floor as the evening wears on.

Rehab Bar and Grill

Popular among the LGBTQ community and renowned for its lively environment is Rehab Bar and Grill in The Grove. The pub has themed events, karaoke nights, and a large outside terrace that draws a vibrant and varied clientele. Rehab provides a friendly environment for everyone, whether you want to sing, dance, or simply hang out with friends.

Soulard

Known for its bustling pub culture and architectural charm, Soulard is one of the oldest districts in St. Louis. Soulard is a must-see location for those who enjoy the nightlife, especially for its lively farmers market and Mardi Gras events.

The Duke's

Duke's is a multi-story restaurant and bar with plenty to offer everyone. There are lots of TVs on the main level to watch sports, while a more laid-back lounge environment can be found in the second story. Duke's third story, "The Upstairs," becomes a nightclub with live DJs and a dance floor for those who want to party all night.

Molly's in Soulard

The well-liked local pub Molly's in Soulard has a large terrace outside that's ideal for pleasant summer evenings. In addition to artisan beers, cocktails, and frozen beverages, the pub has a wide drink menu. Molly's is a popular hangout for both residents and tourists, often hosting live music performances, DJ sets, and special events.

Central West End

Sophisticated nightlife is available in the fashionable and affluent Central West End (CWE). For those seeking a more sophisticated night out, the CWE is the perfect choice with its blend of classy lounges, intimate pubs, and attractive bars.

Dressel's Public House

A quaint and pleasant tavern with a friendly atmosphere is Dressel's Public House. Dressel's is well-known for its large assortment of specialty beers and substantial pub grub, making it an excellent spot to unwind and relax with friends. Locals love this tavern because of its quaint interior design and welcoming staff.

Sub Zero Vodka Bar

Sub Zero Vodka Bar offers more than 500 different types of vodka from throughout the globe, making it one of the biggest collections in the nation. Sushi and beautifully made vodka cocktails may be enjoyed in a stylish atmosphere at this sleek and contemporary bar. You may navigate the bar's large menu with the assistance of its skilled staff, guaranteeing a memorable and pleasurable encounter.

Cherokee Street

Known for its unique blend of clubs, galleries, and stores, Cherokee Street is a center of St. Louis's cultural and creative life. The area is a terrific place to spend a night out because of its creative attitude and dynamic energy.

The Whiskey Ring

With an astonishing assortment of over 200 kinds, The Whiskey Ring is a cozy pub that specializes in whiskey. Whiskey lovers may experience new flavors and enjoy a well-crafted cocktail at the bar, which has a laid-back, private ambiance. The friendly and informed bartenders are always delighted to share their love of whiskey and provide suggestions.

Fortune Teller Bar

Tarot readings, a distinctive combination of handmade drinks, and a whimsical environment can all be found at the eccentric and diverse Fortune Teller Bar. Fresh, regional ingredients are used to create the unique beverages on the bar's menu. A whimsical and ethereal touch to the evening is provided by the bar's in-house tarot reader, who reads fortunes for patrons.

The nightlife in St. Louis is as vibrant and varied as the city itself, with something to suit every taste. Every area offers a different evening experience, from Soulard's historic elegance to The Grove's hip vibe. St. Louis has something for everyone, whether you're dancing the night away at a club, sipping specialty cocktails in a speakeasy, or taking in live music in a neighborhood pub. Discovering the pubs and nightclubs in the city is a must if you want to take in St. Louis' colorful and energetic atmosphere after dark.

Chapter 9

Getting Around St. Louis

While getting around a new city can be thrilling and a little intimidating, St. Louis has a range of transportation choices to ensure that your vacation goes well. Here's all the information you need to travel about Gateway City, from public transportation to ridesharing and bike rentals.

Public Transportation

MetroLink

A quick and easy method to get about St. Louis and its environs is by using the MetroLink light rail system. Lambert-St. Louis International Airport, downtown St. Louis, Forest Park, and the Delmar Loop are just a few of the important locations that MetroLink links with its two lines, the Red Line and the Blue Line.

Fares:
MetroLink rides cost $2.50 each way. A $7.50 Metro Day Pass, which provides unlimited rides on MetroLink and MetroBus for the duration of the day, is a good option if you want to use public transit regularly.

Time:
Depending on the time of day, MetroLink runs trains every 10 to 20 minutes from around 4:00 AM until 1:00 AM.

Accessibility:

Wheelchair accessibility is offered by all MetroLink trains and stops, and each station has an elevator.

MetroBus

With its wide bus service across the city and adjacent suburbs, the MetroBus system is a valuable addition to the MetroLink. MetroBus has more than 70 routes that will transport you almost anywhere in the metropolitan region.

Fares:
MetroBus tickets cost $2.00 for a single journey. Unlimited bus trips are also included with the Metro Day Pass previously stated.

Time:
Although specific schedules differ for each route, the majority of bus lines run from early in the morning until late at night. Make sure to utilize the Transit app or the Metro St. Louis website to get the most recent timetables.

Accessibility:
To assist passengers with impairments, every MetroBus vehicle has lifts or ramps installed.

Downtown Trolley

A convenient and enjoyable way to see the center of St. Louis is on the Downtown Trolley. Along its route, which passes by well-known downtown landmarks including Union Station, the City Museum, and the Gateway Arch, is this vibrantly colored trolley bus.

Fares:
The Downtown Trolley fare is $1.00 per trip; Metro Day Passes are accepted.

Time:
From 10:00 AM to 6:00 PM, seven days a week, the trolley is in operation.

Wheelchair accessibility is available for the Downtown Trolley.

Ride Sharing

In St. Louis, it's common to find ridesharing services like Uber and Lyft. When traveling with luggage or to locations that are difficult to reach by public transportation, these services provide a practical and frequently economical means of getting around the city.

How to Apply:
To request a trip from your present location to your intended destination, download the Uber or Lyft app, register, and submit a request. The estimated fare and arrival time will be displayed on the app.

Fares:
Demand, time of day, and distance all affect fare. Before confirming transport, both applications provide fare estimates.

Taxis

Another means of transportation in St. Louis is via taxis. In crowded locations, you can hail a cab on the street, locate taxi stands at significant hotels and transit hubs, or phone a nearby taxi firm to hail a ride.

Fares:
St. Louis taxi costs normally begin at around $3.50 for the basic fare, with extra fees for each additional mile and waiting time.

Enterprises:
St. Louis County & Yellow Cab and Laclede Cab are two trustworthy cab services in the city.

Automobile Rentals

Car rentals might be a smart choice if you value the freedom that comes with owning a car. In the city and at Lambert-St. Louis International Airport, there are several vehicle rental companies.

Big firms:
Hertz, Enterprise, Avis, Budget, and Alamo are a few of the big St. Louis-based car rental firms.

Requirements:
A valid driver's license, a credit card, and at least 21 years old are needed to hire a car (age restrictions and prices may vary by business).

Parking:
There are a variety of metered street parking, public parking lots, and garages available in St. Louis. On Sundays and weekdays after 7:00 PM, metered parking is free. To prevent fines, be aware of parking laws and time limitations.

Biking and Scooters

A developing network of bike lanes and trails is making St. Louis a more bike-friendly city. There are plenty of bike rental and bike-sharing options throughout the city, making biking an excellent way to see it at your leisure.

Bike Rental:

Big Shark Bicycle Company:
For those who want to explore the city, this local store rents out bikes. They give an assortment of bikes, such as electric, hybrid, and road cycles.

Forest Park Bike Rentals:
Bicycles may be rented at this Forest Park location and used for leisurely rides throughout the park's numerous attractions.

Bike Sharing:

Lime:
Lime offers dockless electric bikes and scooters all across St. Louis. To unlock it, just download the Lime app, find a bike or scooter nearby, and scan the QR code.

Costs:
To unlock a bike or scooter, pay-as-you-go prices usually start at $1.00 plus an extra fee every minute.

Biking Trails:

Numerous beautiful bike routes can be found in St. Louis, which are ideal for both recreational and competitive riding.

The Grant Trail:
Families and recreational bikers will love this 8-mile paved track. Along the trip, there are historical markers and beautiful scenery as it passes through South and Southwest St. Louis County.

The Riverfront Path:
Starting near the Gateway Arch, this 11-mile path follows the Mississippi River and offers breathtaking views of the river and the cityscape of the city.

Katy's Trail:
The Katy Trail is a 240-mile rail trail across the state of Missouri, perfect for a longer excursion. Although the full path requires several days to complete, the St. Charles segment is conveniently located near St. Louis and provides an exquisite ride through stunning scenery.

Strolling

The Loop, Central West End, and downtown are among the walkable parts of St. Louis. For a close-up look at the city's architecture, parks, and independent stores, walking is frequently the best option.

Downtown St. Louis:

Condensed and brimming with attractions, downtown includes the Gateway Arch, Old Courthouse, and City Garden. It's a lovely and simple stroll between these locations.

Central West End:
This posh area is well-known for its outdoor cafés, chic stores, and ancient residences. It's fun to explore on foot because of the walkable streets.

The Loop:
There are plenty of stores, eateries, and entertainment options on the busy Delmar Loop. It's a terrific spot for a stroll, especially after dark when the neighborhood comes to life with bustle.

Because of its extensive ridesharing network, walkable neighborhoods, and well-designed public transit system, getting to St. Louis is simple and convenient. There are many different ways to get around St. Louis, depending on your preferences: you may explore on foot or by bike, enjoy the convenience of MetroLink and MetroBus, or have the freedom of a rental vehicle. Savor exploring the Gateway City's plethora of sights, sounds, and flavors!

Accommodation Options

Choosing the ideal lodging option may significantly improve your St. Louis trip. From opulent hotels and quaint bed-and-breakfasts to affordable motels and practical vacation rentals, the city provides a broad choice of lodging to fit every taste and budget. An outline of the top lodging choices in St. Louis may be found here.

Opulent Hotels

St. Louis offers several opulent luxury hotels with first-rate facilities, exquisite settings, and outstanding service for visitors looking for a high-end experience.

The Ritz-Carlton, St. Louis:
Situated in the affluent Clayton area, The Ritz-Carlton provides an elegant yet cozy ambiance. Enjoy the large accommodations, exquisite dining at The Grill, a full-service spa, and the hotel's handy location close to Forest Park and downtown.

- Price points: From around $350 per night.

- Features: In-house restaurant, exercise center, spa, and pet-friendly lodging.

Four Seasons Hotel St. Louis:
The Four Seasons Hotel is the height of luxury, located downtown with breathtaking views of the Mississippi River and the Gateway Arch. The hotel has a rooftop pool, a cutting-edge exercise facility, and the well-known Cinder House restaurant, which serves food with influences from South America.

Starting at around $450 per night, the rooftop pool, full-service spa, fitness center, exquisite dining, and event rooms are among the amenities.

Boutique Hotels

Give one of St. Louis's boutique hotels a try for a more distinctive and individualized experience. Personalized service, unique design, and cozy settings are common features of these places.

The Moonrise Hotel:
Situated in The Loop, The Moonrise Hotel blends modern design elements with an entertaining vintage space motif. A well-liked location for drinks and breathtaking city views is the hotel's rooftop patio, which has a luminous sculpture of the moon.

- Costs: From about $180 per night.

- Features: Pet-friendly accommodations, a fitness center, a rooftop bar, and Eclipse Restaurant on-site breakfast.

The Cheshire:
Located next to Forest Park, The Cheshire is a quaint boutique hotel with an English feel. The hotel features many dining options, including Fox & Hounds Tavern and Basso, and each room is distinctively furnished with tributes to British literature and culture.

- Costs: From around $150 per night.

- Features: Free breakfast, pet-friendly accommodations, an outdoor pool, and a variety of on-site eating options.

Mid-Range Hotels

There are several mid-range hotel alternatives available in St. Louis for those seeking a mix of comfort and budget. With a variety of features, these hotels provide good value.

Drury Plaza Hotel St. Louis at the Arch:
The Drury Plaza Hotel, which is close to the Gateway Arch, provides cozy lodgings along with several free features, such as evening refreshments, Wi-Fi, and a hot breakfast.

- Prices: $130 per night and above.

- Amenities: Free breakfast, evening snacks, indoor pool, exercise center, and business center.

Hampton Inn & Suites St. Louis at Forest Park:
Convenient access to Forest Park and its numerous attractions is provided by this contemporary hotel. Comfortable accommodations, a free cooked breakfast, and quick access to St. Louis's downtown are available to guests.

Starting at around $160 per night, the accommodations provide complimentary breakfast, an indoor pool, a fitness facility, and free parking.

Affordable Choices

St. Louis has a range of affordable lodging alternatives that prioritize comfort and convenience for budget-conscious guests.

Red Roof Inn Plus+ St. Louis - Forest Park/Hampton Avenue:

This inexpensive hotel is close to Forest Park and offers reasonably priced, well-kept rooms. For those who want to see the city without going over budget, it's a fantastic choice.

- Costs: Beginning at about $70 per night.

- Amenities: Free parking, pet-friendly accommodations, and free Wi-Fi.

Motel 6 St. Louis - Airport:

This hotel is reasonably priced and provides simple lodging close to Lambert-St. Louis International Airport. For tourists looking for a fast and affordable place to stay, it's perfect.

- Prices: Beginning at around $50 per night.

- Amenities: Complimentary Wi-Fi, complimentary parking, and pet-friendly accommodations.

Bed and Breakfasts

Staying at one of St. Louis's quaint bed & breakfasts will provide you with a warm and comfortable experience. These facilities frequently have more intimate settings, distinctive décor, and individualized service.

Fleur-de-Lys Mansion:

Situated in a superbly refurbished 19th-century estate, the Fleur-de-Lys Mansion provides sophisticated accommodations together with a delectable breakfast every morning. Situated next to Tower Grove Park, it's ideal for an intimate weekend escape.

- Prices: From about $200 per night.

- Amenities: Gourmet breakfast, complimentary WiFi, and opulent accommodations including whirlpool tubs and fireplaces.

Lehmann House Bed & Breakfast:
Nestled in the heart of the historic Lafayette Square district, Lehmann House is a cozy Victorian-style residence. In addition to the elegance of a bygone period, guests may have a substantial prepared breakfast.

- Price Range: From around $150 per night.

- Amenities: Free Wi-Fi, well-equipped accommodation, and a complimentary breakfast are among the amenities offered.

Vacation Rentals

Families or parties may experience a home-away-from-home with additional room and facilities when they rent a vacation. From lofts in the downtown area to houses in the suburbs, well-known websites like Airbnb and Vrbo have a wide range of possibilities in St. Louis.

AirBnb

- Options: Entire St. Louis houses, lofts, and flats are available as options.

- Rates: The prices range greatly, from about $60 for a solitary room to more than $200 for a whole house.

- Amenities: Fully equipped kitchens, coin-operated laundry rooms, and distinctive, regional experiences are among the amenities offered.

Vrbo

- Options: Spacious residences and apartments fit for gatherings of friends or family.

- Rates: Depending on the property's location and size, rates typically begin at around $100 per night and may increase.

- Amenities: Ample bedrooms, kitchens, and frequently outside areas are among the amenities.

A variety of lodging choices are available in St. Louis to accommodate every traveler's preferences and price range. There are several options available in the Gateway City, depending on your preferences: opulence of an upscale hotel, attractiveness of a boutique property, affordability of a low-cost motel, or coziness of a vacation rental. Select the lodging choice that best suits your preferences, and then take advantage of all that St. Louis has to offer while having a cozy stay.

Safety Tips and Traveler Resources

Traveling safely is of utmost importance. Although St. Louis is a friendly and energetic city, you should exercise caution and be alert to your surroundings just as you would in any other metropolitan setting. Here are some helpful links and safety advice to ensure a safe and pleasurable stay.

General Safety Tips

Remember to be Aware of Your Environment:
Always be aware of your surroundings, whether you're taking in the nightlife or seeing the city during the day. Be vigilant with your possessions and refrain from flaunting things in public.

Remain in Well-Lit Areas:
Pick busy, well-lit places to stroll in, especially at night. Steer clear of alleyways and remote areas while taking shortcuts.

Use Reliable Transit:

Make sure the taxis, public transit, and ridesharing services you use—such as Uber and Lyft—are legitimate and authorized. Don't take transportation from unaffiliated providers.

Preserve Personal Items:
To ensure the safety of your possessions, carry a crossbody bag or a bag featuring a zipper. Keep an eye on your phone, wallet, and other valuables when you're in public areas.

Be Aware of Emergency Phone Numbers:
To get help right away in an emergency, phone 911. Knowing the embassy or consulate of your nation's contact details is also beneficial.

Keep Up to Date:
Pay attention to local news and weather reports. Recognize any notices or advisories that might influence your travel schedule.

Neighborhood Safety

There are several different neighborhoods in St. Louis, and each has a unique personality and safety profile. Here are some pointers for traversing various environments:

Downtown St. Louis:
Downtown St. Louis is generally secure throughout the day, particularly in the areas surrounding well-known tourist destinations. At night, stay in well-traveled places and use care.

Central West End:
This district, which is well-known for its lively dining and shopping scene, is safe overall, but be cautious, especially in the less crowded sections.

Soulard:
Soulard, well-known for its vibrant nightlife and historic elegance, is typically secure and busy, although use caution when strolling at night.

The Loop:
A busy neighborhood featuring stores, eateries, and entertainment options is The Loop. It's safe to investigate but proceed with caution as always, especially after nightfall.

Health and Wellness

Excellent healthcare facilities are available in St. Louis, so it's a good idea to know where to go if you need medical attention:

Barnes-Jewish Hospital:
Conveniently placed next to Forest Park, this esteemed hospital in the area.

St. Louis Children's Hospital:
Close to Forest Park, this hospital is well-known for its pediatric services.

An urgent care facility:
The city is home to a large number of urgent care facilities for non-emergency medical conditions.

Traveler Resources

Visitor Centers:
You may obtain maps, brochures, and guidance from knowledgeable locals at several St. Louis tourist centers:

- St. Louis Visitor Center:
  Situated downtown at 701 Convention Plaza, this facility offers extensive help and information.

- The Forest Park Visitor Center provides details about the park's offerings, activities, and events.

Local Services

- Public Wi-Fi: A lot of public areas, including Forest Park, the Gateway Arch grounds, and several libraries, provide free Wi-Fi.

- ATM Locations: The city is full of ATMs, which can be found in hotels, retail centers, and key attractions.

- Language Assistance: Although the official language is English, many lodging facilities and tourist destinations offer multilingual personnel.

Travel Insurance

Think about getting medical costs, vacation cancellations, and lost property covered by travel insurance. In the event of unanticipated circumstances, this might offer financial security and peace of mind.

You may have a worry-free and safe trip to St. Louis by heeding this safety advice and making use of the services that are accessible. Make the most of your time touring Gateway City by being well-informed and prepared. These recommendations can help make sure your vacation is safe and memorable, whether you're visiting the Missouri History Museum to learn about its rich history, admiring the Gateway Arch, or going out on the town in the Central West End.

Made in the USA
Monee, IL
29 October 2024